Life of Jesus

Life of

JESUS

by

François Mauriac

LONDON
HODDER AND STOUGHTON

First published, February 1937
This edition, June 1949

Translated from the French by Julie Kernan

"Christianity dwells essentially in Christ. It is less His doctrine than it is His Person. Therefore the Scriptural texts cannot be detached from Him without at once losing their meaning and their life. Eminent services have been rendered in the *material* study of the books in which the primitive Church summed up its belief, by the sagacity, loyalty and patience of critics; but these qualities—without Faith—could not initiate them into the interior life of the texts, or make them realise the continuity, the movement and the mystery in the light of the Presence which is the soul of these writings."

MAURICE ZUNDEL: *The Poem of the Holy Liturgy*

TABLE OF CONTENTS

CHAPTER VIII

CHAPTER IX

CHAPTER X

CHAPTER XI

CHAPTER XII

CHAPTER XIII

CHAPTER XIV

CHAPTER XV

CHAPTER XVI

CHAPTER XVII

CHAPTER XVIII

CHAPTER XIX

CHAPTER XX

CHAPTER XXVI

CHAPTER XXVII

PREFACE

OF ALL HISTORIANS, the Biblical scholar is the most deceiving. If he belong to the category of those who first deny the supernatural and who do not see the God in Jesus, we may be certain that he understands nothing of the subject of his studies and all his learning is not worth a farthing. On the other hand, if he be a Christian, we may say that too often his very fervour causes the painter's hand to tremble and obscures his vision; the man named Jesus, whose portrait he draws for us, risks being swallowed up in the lightning power of the second Divine Person.

There is no doubt that the union of learning and mystical understanding in certain writers has given rise in France to admirable works like those of Lagrange, de Grandmaison, Lebreton, Pinard de Laboulaye, Huby. But, unfortunately, there are others, and we know why reasonable people have come to-day to deny the historical existence of Christ. The Jesus of the Gospels, at times lowered by historians to the proportions of an ordinary man, at others raised by adoration and love far above the earth where he lived and died, loses, in the eyes of the faithful as in those of the indifferent, all definite outline, and presents none of the features of a real person.

Now it is here that a Catholic writer, even the most ignorant, a novelist—but who knows himself, if I may say so, in heroes of his own invention—has perhaps the right to bring his testimony. No doubt a Life of Jesus should be written on one's knees, with a feeling of unworthiness great enough to make the pen drop from the hand! A sinner should blush for his temerity in undertaking such a work.

But such a writer may at least assure the reader that the Jesus of the Gospels is the contrary of an artificial and composite being. Here is the most moving of the great figures of history, and of all the great

B

characters history places before us, the least logical because he is the most living. It is for us to understand him in what is most peculiar and essential to ourselves.

Before we think of him as God, we must think of him as a man in an epoch fairly near to our own; a definite man belonging to his own country, his own clan, a man among many, one of them—so much, indeed, that to distinguish him from the eleven poor people about him, the kiss of Judas must point him out. This journeyman carpenter speaks and acts as God. This Galilean of the lower classes, member of a very poor family, which family, moreover, mocks him and believes him mad, possesses such power over matter, over bodies and over hearts that he stirs up the people to a fresh hope of the coming of the Messiah; and the priests, to put down the imposter, must have recourse to their worst enemy, the Roman.

Yes, in their eyes, he was an impostor served by demons, a parody of God who pretended to forgive sins and whose blasphemy surpassed all blasphemy. In such guise appeared to them the Jesus whose followers cherished him in trembling, as a friend at once all powerful and all humble; the same men under these two aspects, unique but differing in the hearts that reflected him; adored by the poor and hated by the mighty because of that in him which was divine, and for the rest, misunderstood by one as much as the other. This is the subject of my painting, the portrait I am so foolhardy as to undertake.

A Jesus misunderstood and therefore irritated, impatient, sometimes raging, as is all love. But beneath this surface violence there reigned a deep peace which was his own and which was like no other. *His* peace he called it, the peace of union with the Father, the gentle calm that knew its hour beforehand and saw stretched ahead the road ending in agony, insults and the gibbet.

An apparent violence and an underlying calm is also manifested in his words. They must be gone over one by one, cleansed of the rust of time, of those deposits laid on by long habit, relieved of those layers of assuasive commentary accumulated over a period of nineteen hundred years. Then shall we hear again the voice that is to be confused with no other voice; after so many centuries it still rings in every word of his that has been preserved to us, and will never cease to excite not only love but, as Lacordaire says, "those virtues fructifying in love."

This rash book will not have been written in vain if a single reader, on closing it, suddenly sees the meaning of the words of those guards who were reproached by the high priests for not daring to put hands on Jesus: "Never did man speak as this man speaketh."

I

UNDER THE REIGN of Tiberius Cæsar, the carpenter Ieschou, son of Joseph and Mary, lived in the straggling village, Nazareth, of which there is no mention in history and which the Old Testament does not name; several houses hollowed out in a rocky hillside facing the plain of Esdrelon. Vestiges of these caves are still to be found, and one of them sheltered this child, this boy, this man, together with a workman and the Virgin. There he lived for nearly thirty years, but not in a silence of adoration and love. Jesus dwelt in the thick of a clan, in the midst of the petty talk, the jealousies, the small dramas of his numerous kin, devout Galileans, enemies of Rome and of Herod, who, awaiting the triumph of Israel, went up to Jerusalem for the feasts.

They were there then from the beginning of his hidden life— those who, at the time of his first miracles, were to claim he was out of his mind and who wished to lay hands on him; those whose names are given us in the Gospel: James, Joseph, Simon, Jude. . . . To what degree he made himself like all the boys of his age is proved by the scandal of the Nazarenes when for the first time he preached in their synagogue. He could not bring them to believe. "Is not this the carpenter," they said, "the son of Mary, and his brethren [his cousins] . . . are they not all with us?" In this way they spoke of him, these people of the neighbourhood who had seen him grow up, or had played with him, those whose orders he had but lately carried out; he was the carpenter, one of the two or three carpenters of the town.

And yet, as in all the workshops of that humble world, the one of which we speak would, at a certain hour, become dark. The door and the window would be closed against the street. Then those three beings would be alone in the room, round a table on which bread had been placed. A man called Joseph, a woman called Mary, a boy called Ieschou. Later, when Joseph had departed from this world, the son and the mother remained, facing each other, waiting.

What did they say to each other? *"But Mary stored up all these things in her heart and pondered them."* This text from Luke, and another from the same evangelist, *"And his mother stored up all these things in her heart,"* prove not only that he received from Mary all that he knew of the childhood of Christ, but they pierce with a fiery dart the obscurity of the life led by the three, then the two, in the carpenter's shop. Certainly the woman could forget nothing of the mystery consummated in her flesh; but as the years flowed on with the promise of the angel of the Annunciation still unfulfilled, another than she might perhaps have turned her thoughts away, for those prophecies were obscure and terrifying.

Gabriel had said, "And behold, thou shalt conceive in thy womb and shalt bring forth a son; and thou shalt call his name Jesus. He shall be great, and shall be called Son of the Most High; and the Lord God shall give to him the throne of David his father, and he shall reign over the house of Jacob for ever, and of his reign there shall be no end."

Now the child had become a stripling, then a youth, then a man—a Galilean workman bent over his bench. He was not great; he was not called the Son of the Most High; he had no throne but a stool near the fireplace in a poor kitchen. The mother could have doubted. . . . Now here is the testimony of Luke: Mary stored up all these things in her heart and constantly pondered them.

In her heart—she guarded them, she did not betray them, even, perhaps, to her son. A dialogue between the two is hard to imagine. They spoke in Aramaic, the ordinary words of poor people, words designating ordinary objects—tools, food. There were no words for that which was accomplished in this woman.

The family, in silence, contemplated the mystery. Meditation on the mysteries began there, in the shadows of Nazareth where the Trinity breathed.

At the fountain, at the washing-place, whom could the Virgin have made believe she was a virgin and had given birth to the Messiah? But in the course of her tasks, nothing could keep her from pondering over these treasures in her heart; the salutation of the angel, the words pronounced for the first time, "Hail, full of grace, the Lord is with thee: blessed art thou among women . . ." words to be repeated countless times throughout the ages. This the humble Mary knew, when, prompted by the Holy Spirit, she had one day prophesied to her cousin Elizabeth, "all generations shall call me blessed."

After twenty years, after thirty years, did the mother of the carpenter still believe that all generations would call her blessed? She recalled, when she was with child, that journey into the hill country, into a town of Judah. She had gone into the house of the priest Zachary, who was dumb, and of Elizabeth, his wife. And the child carried by the aged woman in her womb had leapt, and Elizabeth had cried, "Blessed art thou among women. . . ."

After twenty years, after thirty years, did Mary still believe herself blessed among women? Nothing had happened, and what could happen to this over-burdened labourer, to this Jew no longer very young, who knew only how to plane boards, to meditate on the Scriptures, to obey and to pray?

Did one single witness remain of those who had assisted from the beginning at God's manifestation on that blessed night in Bethlehem? Where were the shepherds? And those learned men, familiars of the stars, come from beyond the Dead Sea to adore the Child? Then the whole history of the world had seemed to bend itself to the designs of the Eternal. If, in the days of Herod, Cæsar Augustus had ordered the census of the Empire and its vassal lands like Palestine, it was so that a man and a woman might travel the road that went from Nazareth to Jerusalem and to Bethlehem, and because Micah had prophesied, "And thou, Bethlehem, land of Judah, art no wise least among the rulers of Judah; and from thee shall come forth a ruler, who shall tend my people Israel."

The ageing mother of this carpenter workman gazed into the darkness for the angels who in the days after the Annunciation had continued to people her life. It was they who on that holy night had shown the way to the shepherds; and from the depths of the dark cave where Love trembled from cold in a manger, had promised peace on earth to men of good will. Again it was an angel who in a dream had commanded Joseph to take the Child and his mother and fly into Egypt to escape the anger of Herod. . . . But after the return to Nazareth, the heavens had closed, the angels had disappeared.

This was necessary, that the Son of God might become deeply embedded in the flesh of man. From year to year, the mother of the carpenter might have believed she had dreamed, if she had not remained continually in the presence of the Father and of the Son, going over again and again in her heart the things which had come to pass.

THE AGED SIMEON

From only one of these incidents did she sometimes, perhaps, force herself to turn away her thoughts. There had been words pronounced in the Temple which she, at certain times, was tempted to forget. The fortieth day after the birth of the child, they had come back to Jerusalem that Mary might be purified, and that she might present to the Lord the male child who belonged to Him as did every first-born child, and who must be ransomed at the price of five shekels. An old man named Simeon had taken the child in his arms. And suddenly, he burst forth with joy in the Holy Spirit: Might the Lord let him depart in peace now that his eyes had seen the salvation, the light of revelation to nations, the glory of Israel.

. . . But why did the old man turn suddenly to Mary? Why had he prophesied, "Thine own soul a sword shall pierce"?

From that time the words had never left her: those words, that sword. They had entered into her at that hour and remained buried deep in her heart. Because she knew that she could be wounded only through her son, that all suffering, like all joy, could come only through him. This is why what remained in Mary of human weakness rejoiced, perhaps, that the years were passing by and nothing had happened to dispel the obscurity of their poor house and of their humble lives. Perhaps she thought that the only thing needed for the salvation of the world was this presence, unknown to the world, this secret shrouding of God in the flesh—and that she had no other sword to fear than the sorrow of being alone among creatures to witness this immense love.

II

THE CHILD IN THE MIDST OF THE DOCTORS

THIS LIFE was so ordinary, so like other lives, that Luke, who prided himself in opening his Gospel, of having "followed up all things carefully from the beginning," finds nothing to tell of the boyhood of Christ save an incident in the course of a journey to Jerusalem made in his twelfth year, with his parents, for the feast of the Passover. When Mary and Joseph turned back towards Nazareth the child had left them. At first they believed he was with their neighbours and acquaintances, and during one whole day they travelled on without him. Then they became troubled. Having sought him in vain from group to group, they retraced their steps distractedly. For three days, they believed they had lost him and wandered about Jerusalem.

When they finally found him in the temple, seated in the midst of the doctors lost in admiration at his words, they did not think of sharing this admiration, and his mother, for the first time perhaps, reproached him:

"My child, why hast thou done so to us? Behold, thy father and I seek thee sorrowing."

And for the first time, Ieschou did not make the reply that an ordinary child would have made; he did not reply in the tone of an ordinary schoolboy. Without insolence, but as though he had no age, as though he were beyond all age, he questioned them in his turn.

"How is it that ye sought me? Knew ye not that I must needs be in my Father's house?"

They knew it, without knowing it. Luke's testimony is formal: the parents did not understand the words which the child spoke to them. Mary was a mother like other mothers, harassed by little cares and worries—and what mother easily sees into the mystery of a vocation? What mother, at a certain hour, is not baffled before her growing child, who knows where he wants to go? But Mary's predestined spirit, enlightened since the beginning, accepted that which the poor woman did not understand. Nevertheless, these words of her son must have seemed hard to her. Yet did her Ieschou ever say kind words to her until just before the end, when he spoke to her from the height of the cross?

Luke assures us that Jesus was submissive to his parents. He does not add that he was ever tender with them. None of the words of Christ to his mother related in the Gospels (except the last) but show his hard independence of the woman; as if he had made use of her for his incarnation, and having issued from her flesh, there was apparently no longer anything in common between him and her. To those who were one day to say to him, "Thy mother and thy brethren are standing without, seeking to speak to thee . . ." he replied, "Who is my mother, and who are my brethren?" Then casting his eyes over those who were seated about him, "Behold my mother and my brethren! For whosoever doth the will of my Father who is in the heavens, he is my brother and sister and mother."

This at least is certain: the child of twelve spoke to her without kindness, as if he wished to make the distance between them; suddenly he was like a stranger. Mary knew this had to be. Besides, a pressure of the hand, a look, is enough for a mother to know that she is loved; and this mother felt the constant presence of her Son within her. She never had to lose him, never having ceased to bear him in her heart. Christ had all eternity in which to glorify his mother in the flesh. Here below, perhaps he sometimes treated her as he still does his chosen ones whom he has marked for holiness and who, behind their grilles, in their cells, or in the midst of the world, know all the appearances of abandon, of being forsaken, not without keeping the interior certainty of being his elect and beloved.

This Jesus of twelve, who grew in wisdom, in age and in grace, and who on leaving Jerusalem his mother had believed to be in the company of kinsfolk and neighbours, was thus thrown with many people, artisans like himself, or labourers, workers in the vineyards, lake fishermen—people who talked of sowing, of sheep, of nets, of boats and fish, who gazed at the setting sun to foretell the wind or rain. He knew even then that to be understood by simple men he must use words that meant things that daily they handled, gathered, sowed, or harvested in the sweat of their brow. And even that which surpasses these things is understood by poor people only in comparison with them or by analogy: the water in the well, wine, grain of mustard-seed, the fig-tree, sheep, a little leaven, a measure of flour—this is all the humble need in order to understand the truth.

THE YOUNG MAN JESUS

A Jewish boy of twelve had already put his childhood behind him. This Jesus who astonished the doctors must have appeared to the Nazarenes a very pious boy versed in the knowledge of the Torah. But between the incident in the journey to Jerusalem and his entrance into the arena, into the full light, eighteen mysterious years flowed by. Because childhood is sometimes so pure a thing the child Jesus is imaginable; but how can we picture Jesus the young man? Jesus the man?

How can we pierce this darkness? He was fully man, and, except for sin, he had taken on all our infirmities, our youth also, but doubtless without that restlessness, that ever-disappointed eagerness, that agitation of heart. When he was thirty it would be enough for him to say to a man, "Leave all and follow me," for that man to rise and follow him. Women would renounce their folly to adore him. His enemies were to hate in him the man who fascinated and seduced, for beings who are not loved call others seducers. Nothing of this power over hearts yet showed, perhaps, in the boy who planed boards and meditated on the Torah, in the midst of a human little group of artisans, of peasants and fishermen. But what do we know of this? Even though covered with ashes, did there not smoulder in his look and his voice the fire he had come to light on earth? Perhaps there were young men to whom he said, "Rise not; do not follow me."

What did they say of him? Why did the son of the carpenter not take a wife? Perhaps it was his piety which forbade. Uninterrupted prayer, although not manifested by words, creates about the holy an atmosphere of peaceful contemplation and adoration. We have all known beings who, busied with ordinary tasks, remain constantly in the presence of God; and the vilest men respected them, sensing this presence in an obscure way.

In truth, he who would one day cause the wind and the sea to obey him, had also the power to cause a great peace to reign over hearts. He had the power to prevent women from being troubled at sight of him; he could appease the rising tempest because it was not the Son of God who would have been adored in him, but a child among the sons of man.

III

THE EXCITEMENT raised by the preaching of John the Baptist reached Nazareth. If there existed, in the fifteenth year of the reign of Tiberius, a corner of the world where men knew what the only true God expects and demands of each of us in particular—not sacrifices or holocausts, but interior purity, contrition of heart, humility, love of the poor—it was in the Galilee ruled by Herod Antipas the tetrarch, among those people distrusted by the Greeks and Romans. Athens and Rome had advanced as far as it was possible to go, in domination, in knowledge and in enjoyment. Here, a little people struck out in the opposite direction, turned their backs on the quest for power, for satiety and sensual satisfaction. Upon the shores of the Dead Sea the Essenes lived, abstinent and chaste, concerned only with their souls.

We can imagine, in his workshop in Nazareth, the man watching for his hour that was soon to come. Perhaps Mary spoke to him of John, of the son of her cousin Elizabeth, and of his mysterious birth. Zachary the priest and his wife Elizabeth who was barren, had already reached old age. It was revealed to Zachary while he was alone within the sanctuary offering incense and while the people waited without, that a male child would be born to him, and this child would be filled with the Holy Spirit. Because Zachary had doubted the possibility of this miracle for only a moment, he was stricken dumb until the prediction had come to pass and the aged Elizabeth had brought forth a child. Then against the advice of the neighbours the father had written on a tablet, "John is his name." And at once his tongue was loosened. Mary remembered the visit to her cousin she made six months later. But now after so many years, the canticle she had sung upon the threshold did not rise again from her heart, "*My soul doth magnify the Lord, and my spirit hath exulted in God my Saviour—because he hath regarded the lowliness of his handmaid—yea, behold, henceforth all generations shall call me Blessed.*" No, the silence of the last hours of the hidden life could not be troubled by the hymn of joy. Mary understood that the time had come; the sword was already moving a little.

For the Baptist, who, they said, was clothed in camel's hair and wore a leathern girdle about his loins, and who fed on locusts and wild honey, was not content with preaching penance with threats, nor with baptising by water, but he announced the early arrival of a stranger, "the strap of whose sandals I am not worthy to stoop and loose. . . . I have baptised you with water, and he shall baptise you with the Holy Spirit . . . in the midst of you standeth one whom ye know not."

Publicans, soldiers, the common people put questions to him, "What then are we to do?" He answered the tax-collector, "Exact no more than hath been appointed you," and he commanded the soldiers to refrain from violence. And no doubt these burning hearts were disappointed, those who were soon to receive from another the staggering answer, "If thou wilt be perfect, go, sell what thou hast . . . and come follow me."

John the Baptist spoke openly of this stranger, "He who cometh after me is mightier than I. . . . His winnowing-fan is in his hand, and he will clean out his threshing floor; he will gather his wheat into the barn, but will burn up the chaff with unquenchable fire."

The last days of the hidden life: the workman is no longer a workman; he refuses all orders and the workshop takes on an abandoned air. He had always prayed, but now, day and night, Mary would come upon him, his face against the earth. Perhaps he was already seized with impatience that all be accomplished, impatience which he showed so often during the three years of his ascent to Calvary. Ah! how he longed to hear the first crackling of that fire he had come to light! Until that hour, God had so far sunk himself in man that even his mother, although the mystery had been made known to her, had forgotten it, and allowed herself to rest beneath the weight of her crushing knowledge; he was her child, like other children, whose brow she kissed, over whose sleep she watched, a young man whose tunic she mended. He earned his bread, seated himself at table to eat his meals, talked with the neighbours; and there was no lack of other artisans pious like himself and versed in the Scriptures. No doubt he was the same man who, during those last days, went to the door, listening with an absent expression, without comment, to what the people said, but attentive to the rumours concerning John, now coming from every quarter. Already a power was manifesting itself in him which his mother was alone to see. Yes, a man, or rather "the man," he who was designated by the mysterious name "the Son of Man."

Already he was far away, his thoughts entirely on what he loved, on humanity which he must win—from what an enemy! When he thought of his enemies, Jesus did not think of the Pharisees, the princes of the priests, the soldiers who would strike him in the face. Let us dare to look the truth in the face: he knew his adversary. His adversary has several names in every language. Jesus was the light come into a world delivered over to the powers of darkness. The devil was the apparent master of the universe in the fifteenth year of the rule of Tiberius. He invented for Cæsar in Capri the impious games of which Suetonius tells us. He made use of the gods to corrupt men, he substituted himself for those gods, he deified crime, he was the king of the world.

Jesus knew him, and he did not yet know Jesus; he would not have led him into temptation had he known him. He merely roamed about the purest and holiest soul he had ever dared to approach. But what saint is not fallible? This thought reassured the Cursed One. Did not pride, the cause of his own downfall, show itself like an ulcer on the faces of many who believed themselves angelic?

At this moment of his life, the Son of Man was the gladiator still hidden in obscurity, but about to enter the blinding arena—the fighter awaited and feared by the beast. "I beheld," Christ was to cry one day in exaltation, "I beheld Satan fall like a lightning-flash from heaven." It was perhaps during those last hours of the hidden life that he had the vision of that fall. Did he also see (and how could he not have seen!) that the vanquished archangel carried in his wake millions of souls, more numerous and thickly falling than the flakes of a snow-storm?

He took a cloak, he tied on his sandals. To his mother he said the words of farewell that we shall never know.

IV

HE HASTENED first towards Judæa, towards that region of the Jordan near Bethany where his first friends awaited him and which is not the same Bethany where, a little before his darkest hour, his last friends were to adore him.

Did he journey alone or was he accompanied by other Nazarenes attracted by the baptism of John? In his heart he knew those disciples of the Baptist who came from Bethsaida to Bethany, and knew that he was to charm them away from the Precursor as soon as they had seen him; and that among them was the most beloved of all, the son of Zebedee.

But at first John the Baptist was alone when Jesus approached him; he did not yet know him. It was only later that he was to cry, "Behold the Lamb of God, who taketh away the sins of the world." Jesus came to submit himself to the rites of baptism like any other pious Israelite, as if he had sins to wash away. It was necessary for the Son of Man to make this first gesture that he might emerge from beneath that humanity in which for more than thirty years he had been more hidden than seed in the earth, more hidden than he is to-day in the Eucharist. But it was not for him to cry out: "I am Christ, the Son of God." He cast off his garments to enter the water, despite John's reluctance to baptise him. And then the Spirit covered him visibly with wings whose shadow had hovered thirty years earlier over the Virgin that she might be with child. John the Baptist heard a voice (perhaps others heard it also): "This is my beloved Son. . . ." And then the Son of Man retired into the solitary place where the devil roamed and tormented the formidable stranger.

THE FIRST CALL

After forty days of fasting and meditation, he returned to the place of his baptism. He knew in advance whom he was to meet. "The Lamb of God," said the prophet as he saw him come (and doubtless half aloud). This time two of John's disciples were with him. They looked at Jesus . . . it sufficed! They followed him to the place where he dwelt. One of the two was Andrew, the brother of Simon; the other was John, son of Zebedee. "Jesus looked on him and loved him. . . ." That which is written concerning the rich young man who was to go away sorrowful was doubtless true in regard to John. What did Jesus do to keep them? "Jesus turning round and seeing that they followed him, saith to them, 'What seek ye?' They said to him, 'Rabbi . . . where abidest thou?' He saith to them, 'Come and ye shall see.' They went therefore and saw where he abode, and they abode with him that day; it was about the tenth hour."

The text of the gospel narrative is as moving as any direct words of Christ. The place where he abode? The desert peopled with stones that Satan dared him to turn into bread. That which passed between them at that first meeting, in the dawn of Bethany, was the secret of a more than human love, love inexpressible. Already the lighted fire was catching from tree to tree, from soul to soul. Andrew told his brother that he had found the Christ and brought back to the desert with him Simon, who from that day forward Christ called Kephas.

The next day the conflagration spread, reached Philip, a native of Bethsaida, as were Andrew and Peter. The words and acts which attached him to Christ are not known to us. But the flame spread from Philip to Nathanael. This new tree did not take fire at once, for Nathanael was versed in the Scripture and protested that nothing good could come out of Nazareth. His friend answered simply, "Come and see."

Was it enough for each of these chosen souls to see Jesus in order to recognise him? No, Jesus gave each a sign; and the sign he gave Nathanael was the same he was soon to use to convince the Samaritan woman. "Whence dost thou know me?" Nathanael had asked in a distrustful tone. "Before Philip called thee, when thou wast under the fig-tree, I saw thee." Nathanael at once replied, "Thou art the Son of God."

It matters little that the secret act which took place beneath the fig-tree was never revealed. What Nathanael discovered was that the very depths of his being were known to this man; he felt himself open before him as do the least of us to-day, kneeling for the avowal of our sins or with our faces turned toward the Host. During his mortal life Christ was prodigal of that sign which caused many a simple and unaffected being to fall with his face against the earth. He replied even to the most secret thoughts of the scribes and the Pharisees; but they, far from striking their breasts, saw therein but a ruse of Beelzebub. The faith of the humble Nathanael surprised Christ more than their incredulity, and we may imagine his smile as he said, "Because I said to thee, 'I saw thee under the fig-tree,' thou believest. Greater things than these shalt thou see. . . ."

Perhaps when this encounter with Nathanael took place, Jesus had already left the desert where during forty days he had fasted and suffered the attacks of the Prince of evil. Going up the Jordan by Archelais and Scythopolis, he had reached the lake of Tiberius and Bethsaida, the native country of the disciples who had left John to follow him. Not that the hour of total abandon had as yet sounded for them. Their nets and their barques were still to hold them for a little while; they had had only the first call.

There is nothing to enlighten us concerning the feelings of the abandoned Precursor, except perhaps a certain hostility which was soon to be manifested among the followers of John in regard to the disciples of Jesus. But the Son of Man, who comes as a thief, does not turn his head toward those he has left solitary after taking from them a loved one. His grace acts in the secret places of hearts he has deprived of a son, of a daughter; his consolations come in other ways than those which are familiar to us. Nothing is more foreign to him than protestations, excuses, tears. Across centuries of insipidity, we must distinguish this Jewish man, gently implacable, who came to separate, as he himself said, and who set out to do this from the first, with (apparently) a divine indifference for the Precursor, the Baptist whose dearest friends he took away. Soon he was to cry this aloud from the roof-tops: he brought not peace but a sword, he exacted preference to the nearest relatives and even to a master like the Precursor, and required that all these be left to follow him.

V

CANA

IT WAS THIS JESUS, still pale from his fast and struggles with Lucifer, who, following the Jordan, came to the lake of Tiberias with his new friends. And one of them was John, son of Zebedee, already more loved than the others; then Andrew, Simon Peter, Nathanael (now called Bartholomew). Each one of them saw for the first time the drama which Christ introduced into the world and which is played to-day wherever the name of Jesus is glorified: a vocation, the call, the struggle of poor men engaged in the midst of life, harassed by a thousand obstacles, held back above all by ties of blood which bind the heart, and committed to an extra-ordinary degree of purity. But on the banks of the lake, those men had the happiness of being alone with Christ. There was no one between them and the Master who drew them to him; no one assumed the prerogative of grace.

Jesus did not hurry them; he left them for a little while with their families, their work, while he rejoined his mother in the house at Nazareth. They were all to meet again at Cana, in Galilee, where they were invited to a wedding. St. John expressly states that Christ went there with his disciples. But as, during the feast, Jesus said to Mary, "My hour is not yet come," we must think of the feast as taking place after his return to Galilee, a little before the apostles had left all to follow him.

Christ's first miracle was performed at the celebration of an earthly union, at a wedding so joyous that the wine failed, and he had to change into wine the water in six stone jars intended for the ablutions!

"He manifested his glory," writes John, "and his disciples believed in him." It was then for their benefit he performed this act, to prepare them to reply to a second call by the complete gift of themselves. It was also because Mary said to him, "They have no wine," and despite his rather hard words, he betrayed on this occasion a divine weakness in regard to his mother.

Already he had begun his habit of crossing every threshold, of sitting at every table, because it was for sinners he came, for those who were lost.

The scandal began at Cana, and lasted until Bethany, up to the time of the last anointing. The man who called himself the Son of God went every day among publicans, courtesans, the dissolute, the derelict. At Cana there were those who lived riotously and could not forgo jests and laughter. The steward of the feast said to the bridegroom, "Every man setteth forth good wine first, and after they have drunk freely then that which is poorer; but thou hast kept the good wine until now." It is impossible to doubt that the contents of the six stone jars added to the joy of a wedding party already well filled with wine. More than one abstemious person put to Christ the hypocritical question which came up so often in the talk of the Pharisees, "Why do the disciples of John fast . . . while thy disciples do not fast?" But he smiled and was silent because his hour was not yet come.

Nevertheless, as he had been warned, Nathanael was the witness of a miracle more astonishing than that which had so amazed him at Bethany; what would the Son of Man not do thenceforth? The day he affirmed that wine was his blood and bread his flesh, those who had been at Cana would not be the last to believe. This first miracle, in appearance the least "spiritual" of all, prepared them for what was to come, introduced them to the unimaginable mystery.

THE FINAL CALL

Jesus, with his followers, went to Capharnaum, to the shores of the lake where Simon, Andrew, James and John found once more their boats and their nets. His grip on them loosened for a little while; they would never escape him again. We have read the story so often it seems simple to us that Jesus, passing along the shores of the lake and seeing his friends cast down their nets, had need of only the words, "Come, follow me and I will make you fishers of men," for them, without so much as a turn of the head, to leave all and follow him. However, it was not without his having given them a new sign of his power, chosen from among all those which might most surely strike these simple minds. He had first borrowed their boat in order to escape the people who pressed too closely upon him. Simon had rowed out a little way, and Jesus, seated in the stern, spoke to the multitude grouped about the water's edge, to a multitude in which feeling ran high, for already there was great division of opinion concerning him. In Nazareth, in the synagogue (where like any pious Jew he had the right to speak) his commentaries of the prophecies had irritated the people who had known him from his earliest years. To them the carpenter Ieschou was of little importance, despite the cures which were beginning to be laid at his door. Their irritation had reached its height when he had let them understand that the Gentiles would be preferred to them, and it was only by a miracle he had escaped their fury.

Now he no longer risked being alone; here he was in the boat with Simon and the sons of Zebedee. Since that day in Bethany, these boatmen knew that he saw into the secret life of each one of them; they had seen with their own eyes the miracle of Cana; Jesus had cured Simon's mother-in-law of fever. It remained for him to touch them in that which counted for most in their eyes: to catch as many fish as they wished—it was their job to know that was extremely difficult. Indeed, they had worked all that night without catching anything. And now Simon had to call James and John to his help to draw in the nets. The two boats were so full of fish they were almost sinking. Then Kephas fell to his knees. To-day still it is a sign that God is present, when we see our own defilement in all its horror. "Depart from me, for I am a sinful man, O Lord." Jesus' answer, like many of his words, contained a prophecy which we are still seeing fulfilled before our eyes: "Henceforth thou shalt catch men."

Nevertheless, at least one of them, Simon, was married. And when they received the final call, James and John left not only their boat, but Zebedee, their father. They left him "with the hired men," the Evangelist specifies, to stress the full horror of this abandonment. "If anyone come unto me," Jesus was to repeat one day with singular violence, "and hate not his father and mother, and wife and children, and brothers and sisters, yea, and his very life, he cannot be my disciple." Never had the Son of Man insisted with such vehemence on a demand so contrary to nature. Yet this unheard-of requirement was not at the end, but the beginning of all sanctification. No, it was not without reason that as much as Christ was loved he was also violently hated. It is childish to be scandalised because many who saw Christ in the flesh could not love him! Many persons qualify his most stinging words as hyperbole; all orientals have an excessive language. And yet "this is a hard saying," said the Jews, "who can listen to it." It still appears just as hard, just as hateful to us. Absolute love repels the mediocre, shocks the self-satisfied, disgusts the fastidious. Doubtless his enemies would hate him much more than they do (and his pretended friends also) if they had not for so many centuries substituted the pale and insipid Rabbi pictured to-day for the man who really lived and showed himself a character "integrated" in the metaphysical sense. It is ignorance which to-day keeps many from detesting Christ. If they knew him, they could not abide him.

Jesus had so far weighed his words that he warned us to test our strength before trying to follow him. "For," said he, "which of you, if he would build a tower, doth not first sit down and count the cost, whether he have wherewith to complete it? Lest perchance if he have laid the foundation and cannot finish, all who behold begin to mock him saying, 'This man began to build and cannot finish. . . .' " It is the story of all the false yearnings toward God. It is so easy to be converted, to be pardoned! But Christ himself asks us first to be sure of our powers knowing whence he leads us and how high a price he paid for his love of us.

VI

AFTER A BRIEF STAY at Capharnaum, where through the mouths of those possessed, the devil cried out against him, where the sick besieged him on every side, he went up to Jerusalem, for it was the Passover and the time of the great sacrifice. For the rich, merchants brought flocks of oxen and of sheep on to the porches of the temple. Others sold the doves that were sacrificed by the poor. The money-changers were there at the disposal of those who had need of their services. What could be more simple, and what was scandalous in it? *Since it is for God*—the eternal little excuse. Suddenly he came in, a furious man, armed with a whip, not a child's whip, but one made with cords. His dumbfounded disciples refrained from following his example. He cast out the animals, overturned the tables, crying, "Take them away! Make not of the house of my Father a house of traffic!" What scandal! The cowards fled after their beasts. Even his friends did not know that He was Love. Beneath this outburst who could discern the love of the Son for the Father?

He must have stopped breathless, his face furious and covered with sweat. The Jews muttered, "What sign dost thou show us, seeing that thou dost these things?" Jesus looked at them. He could have done before their eyes whatever they asked, he could have cured all the sick who were there, drawn from every quarter, besieging him like flies. No doubt he would have done so if one of those cripples had been bold enough to come forth from the multitude and to implore him; but all trembled before the doctors of the Law—before him also, perhaps, as he stood there still shaking, with the cords held in his clenched fist.

Then he turned towards his enemies—Pharisees, doctors, priests. He smiled a little and said, "Destroy this temple, and in three days I will raise it up." At last! He was caught in the very act of irreverence and falsehood. They believed that this man was grossly mocking them. Jesus was speaking of the temple of his body. But even if they had been in good faith (and most of them doubtless were), which of his questioners could have understood him? Did Christ purposely lead them astray? He could not have wished them to listen and not understand, and to look and see nothing. He blinded them because they deserved darkness. They deserved darkness because they had it in their power not to be blind.

"Destroy this temple, and in three days I will raise it up!" The doctors, Pharisees and those who held to the letter of the law exchanged glances and rejoiced. Two of them kept these odious words in their memories; they would recall them on the day of justice, in three years, when the Son of Man would be delivered over to them, and when, gathered about the high priest, they would seek to bear witness against the impostor. Perhaps Jesus, at that moment when he still held in his hand the corded whip, was thinking of the time when later in his life those two would appear to bear witness against him. "This man said, 'I can overthrow the temple of God, and after three days build it up.'" Perhaps in his heart he already heard the question of the high priest, "Answerest thou naught? What is it these men allege against thee?"

NICODEMUS

But the hour of darkness had not yet sounded. The Pharisees who surrounded the Son of Man were not all foxes. It was not enough to be a Pharisee to incur his hatred. One of them, a member of the great council, a teacher of Israel, was troubled by what he heard and saw. He wished to have speech with the stranger. Only there were his brother doctors, his career . . . an upright soul, no doubt, was Nicodemus, but of a different race from the Galilean fishermen who in following their Master had nought to lose save their aged boat and their mended nets. A teacher of Israel had to be more prudent than the common people. Prudence is a virtue, and it is not good to give scandal when one occupies so prominent a position.

And yet Nicodemus could not resist this temptation, this attraction. Not the least of Jesus' miracles was to have disturbed a man so highly placed. In the midst of the night the great personage came to Jesus, and he was not driven away. And since he was a teacher of Israel, the truth was revealed to him in its fullest extent.

Here appears that brand of stupidity peculiar to certain professional philosophers. The Son of Man found himself on a common footing with sinners, with publicans, with lost women, but the learned Nicodemus disconcerted him by the childishness of his logic. "How can a man be born when he is already old? Can he enter into his mother's womb and be born a second time?" this learned man answered him who brought to him the secret of all spiritual life: to die in the flesh in order to live again according to the spirit.

Prudently, Nicodemus retired before dawn. But he was following the Light. Timid and fearful by nature, holding a recognised position, his heart was none the less touched. Grace worked within him slowly, over a period of years, until the day when, timidly, he made bold to come to the defence of the Nazarene before the whole council—until the hour of darkness when he at last found himself, and the perfume which Magdalene poured over the living Lord he was to pour, without further fear of the Jews, over the dead and broken body of his God. And in the secret of the night, when Nicodemus first came, Jesus breathed an odour of aloes and of myrrh.

VII

IN THOSE DAYS difficulties arose between the disciples of John and those of Jesus. John was baptising near Salem. Jesus himself did not baptise, but he did not prevent his disciples from doing so, and they attracted people in greater numbers than the Baptist. The latter tried to appease his followers with the sublime words, "He who hath the bride is the bridegroom; but the friend of the bridegroom, who standeth and heareth him, with joy rejoiceth at the bridegroom's voice. This therefore my joy is fulfilled . . . he must increase, but I must decrease."

Nevertheless, it was the Son of Man who left the field to him. In order to return into Galilee, Jesus could have followed the Jordan as he did on his last return, as did almost all the Jews anxious to avoid Samaria, a region despised and accursed since the Assyrian colonists had brought their idols there. The Samaritans had done worse; they had harboured a renegade priest expelled from Jerusalem, and he had built an altar on Mount Garizim.

If Jesus followed the road, through the ripening fields of Samaria, it was to meet a soul, no less defiled nor better disposed than most. Yet for this soul, and not for another, he entered the enemy territory—the first he was to meet, and the soul he was to use in order to reach many others. Near the little town of Sychar he was overcome with weariness, and he sat down by the well which Jacob had dug. His disciples went away to buy bread; he awaited their return.

The first person to come . . . it happened to be a woman. There were many reasons that Jesus might not have spoken to her. First, it was not becoming for a man to speak to a woman on the road. And then he was a Jew and she was a Samaritan. And then he who knew hearts, and bodies too, was not unaware of the identity of this graceful being.

It was the Man-God who raised his eyes towards this woman. He, infinite Purity, who had no need to put down desire in its lower and more sordid forms, was none the less incarnate desire, since he was incarnate love. He violently desired the soul of this woman. He wished it with an avidity which suffered neither waiting nor delay—at once, at the instant, and even in that place.

The Son of Man demanded the possession of this creature. She might fully be what she was: a concubine, a woman who had dragged in the mud, who passed from one to another, who had lain in the arms of six men, and he whose thing she now was, and who tasted pleasure with her, was not her husband. Jesus took what he found, gathered up no matter what, that his kingdom might come. He looked at her and decided that on that very day this creature would seize Sychar in his name and would found in Samaria the kingdom of God. One whole night he had spent questioning and answering a doctor of the law, trying to make him understand what it meant to die and be born again. The woman who had had six husbands understood at once what the theologian had failed to grasp. Jesus looked at her closely; he had not that haughty air, that contraction of the virtuous before a woman who made a business of love. Neither did he look at her with indulgence nor with connivance. She was a soul, the first to come, of which he was going to make use. A ray of sun lay across a potsherd in the dirt-heap, the flame leaped up, and all the forest caught fire.

The sixth hour. It was hot. The woman heard someone call her. Was the Jew speaking to her? But yes; he said, "Give me to drink." At once coy and mocking, she replied to the perspiring stranger:

"How dost thou, being a Jew, ask to drink of me, who am a Samaritan?"

"If thou didst know the gift of God, and who he is who saith to thee, 'Give me to drink,' thou wouldst have asked of him, and he would have given thee living water."

Christ brooked no delay; his words were incomprehensible to the

Samaritan woman, but like a thief he had already entered into that dark soul. She must have felt besieged on every side, and the stranger whose dripping face and dusty feet she saw before her entered into her soul, invaded her, and she was powerless before this living surge. Dumbfounded, she ceased to mock, and like many women, began to ask childish questions:

"Sir, thou hast no pail and the well is deep; whence then hast thou living water? art thou greater than our father Jacob, who gave us this well, and drank thereof himself, and his sons and his cattle?"

Jesus had no time to lose; he was going to thrust her, with an impatient gesture, into the full glare of the truth. He said:

"Every one that drinketh of this water shall thirst again; but whosoever drinketh of the water that I shall give him shall never thirst, but the water that I shall give him shall become in him a fountain of water springing up unto everlasting life."

Every word of the Lord should be taken to the letter. That is why many have believed themselves drunk with water and have been deceived; this was not the water of which Jesus spoke, since having drunk of it they thirsted again. Nevertheless, the woman replied:

"Sir, give me this water, that I may not thirst, nor come hither to draw."

"Go, call thy husband and come hither."

Always the same methods to persuade the simple; the same method he used with Nathanael when he said, "I saw thee under the fig-tree." It revealed to them at once his knowledge of their lives, or rather his power to take up his abode within them, to enter into their most secret being; and that is why when the Samaritan woman said. "I have no husband," he replied:

"Thou hast said rightly, 'I have no huband'; for thou hast had five husbands, and now he whom thou hast is not thy husband. This hast thou said truly."

The woman did not belong to the royal race of Nathanael and Simon, of those who immediately fell on their knees and struck their breasts. She was at first only a guilty woman caught in her sin, and, in order to divert the attention of this Rabbi who knew too much, she tried to put the discussion on a theological basis. After having stammered, "Sir, I perceive that thou art a prophet . . ." she added hastily:

"Our fathers worshipped on this mountain; yet ye say that the right place for worship is Jerusalem."

Jesus did not allow himself to be turned away; he laid aside the objection with several words. But he was pressed for time; the disciples were returning with provisions. He heard them talking and laughing. They must not come there until he had finished. The truth must be given this poor woman at once.

"The hour cometh and now is, when true worshippers shall worship the Father in spirit and truth. For indeed the Father seeketh such worshippers. God is a spirit; and those who worship him must worship in spirit and truth."

And the Samaritan woman:

"I know that Messiah is coming; when he cometh, he shall declare unto us all things."

Already the disciples' steps could be heard on the road. To hear the secret he had never yet told anyone, Jesus chose this woman who had had five husbands and who then had a lover.

"I that speak with thee am he."

And at that very moment the light of grace was given to the miserable woman, so strong it was that no doubt could even assail her. Yes, this poor burdened Jew who had walked far in the sun and the dust and who so suffered from thirst that he must beg a little water from a woman of Samaria, was the Messiah, the Saviour of the world.

She stood there petrified, until she heard the voices of those who accompanied this man, coming nearer. Then she started to run, like one whose garments were on fire. She entered Sychar to arouse the people. She cried:

"Come and see a man who hath told me all that I have done."

One would have said that Christ, still seated on the edge of the well, while his disciples gave him a morsel of bread, had trouble in returning to their narrow world. "Rabbi, eat!" they insisted. But incarnate love, unmasked by this woman, had not yet had time to become a man again, a man who hungered and thirsted.

"I have food to eat that ye know not."

This answer still came from another world. The poor people imagined that someone had brought him mysterious food to eat. He looked at their staring eyes, their gaping mouths, and beyond in the blinding light the harvest-field of Samaria, with their ripening ears of corn. Above the corn, heads were moving: a troop of people led on by the woman (her lover was perhaps among them!).

Finally, Jesus touched earth again. He spoke of the things of the soil which they knew, quoted a proverb, reassured them, led them to understand that they would reap what he had sown. He had already made them fishers of men, now they would be harvesters of human sheaves.

He tarried for two days in the midst of the outcast Samaritans, thus giving his followers an example which was to be transmitted in vain to the rest of the world. For if there is a part of the Christian message which men have refused and rejected with invincible obstinacy, it is faith in the equal value of all souls, of all races, before the Father who is in heaven.

D

VIII

THY SINS ARE FORGIVEN

HARDLY HAD HE RETURNED to Galilee when stories of his powers spread like wildfire; so that for the time being the Pharisees renounced a direct attack. But they could still hope to find him in error. What was easier for these casuists, whose delight it was to split hairs over the subtleties of the Torah? Especially as he did not seek to avoid their snare, and even went out of his way to fall into it. But he remained unassailable because the motives of his acts escaped them. What was he striving for? What did he seek? Whatever they might think of him, they had not yet imagined that crime inconceivable to a Jew: being a man to make himself God. That in all events would have been too much! And yet . . .

We must forget all we know of Jesus, all that has been accomplished on earth in his name; we must put ourselves in the place of one of those doctors come from Jerusalem or living in Capharnaum. They observed this agitator at close range, because the people drew aside before them, and they found themselves carried forward to the front rank. A certain scribe I am imagining, mixing with others more important than himself, finally found himself inside the house where Jesus was, besieged by the multitude. . . . The human wave had closed behind him, and some men carrying a paralytic sought in vain to open a passage. Doubtless they had come from far, at the price of much fatigue. They would not leave without seeing him they sought. They would wait, cost what it might. Finally, in desperation, they hoisted the sick man to the roof upon his pallet: they took away the tiles and lowered their burden into the room where Jesus was seated and, no doubt, as they did so they provoked protests, furious cries and threats.

The scribe watched the healer, his eyes fixed upon his lips, his hands. Now the words he came in time to hear were most strange and unexpected, for they happened to have nothing to do with the state of the sick man. Or rather it was as though the reply suddenly became understandable in a silent dialogue between the Son of Man and this stricken creature: *"Be of good heart, my child; thy sins are forgiven."*

Many poor souls, face to face with Jesus in those days when he was in the flesh, felt what they would experience to-day in the presence of the Host; they suddenly realised their defilement in all its depth and extent; they saw themselves. The first grace to be received was the grace of lucidity. Hence the cry of Simon, "Depart from me, for I am a sinful man, O Lord!" It was without doubt the same mute prayer that the paralytic offered. He did not say, "Cure me!" but, "Forgive!" And then came the most astonishing words ever to be uttered by human mouth, *"Thy sins are forgiven."*

All the sins of a poor human life, the great and the little, the most shameful, those which could be confided to no one, those which were not only ignoble but ridiculous—and that other sin which it was impossible to forget and yet on which he never allowed his thoughts to rest. All were wiped out, without need of details, without indignation, without any expression of disgust. The Son of Man did not oblige the penitent to dwell upon his shame. He had already lifted him up, far from the crowd which hemmed him in, so that to his own mind the cure of his soul would matter more than the cure of his body.

This time the Pharisees understood at once the meaning of these extraordinary words. They did not dare to express their indignation aloud. Words failed them; they exchanged looks and thought, "Who can forgive sins save God alone?" The blasphemy was so great they did not yet dare to cry blasphemy. But already the Son of Man had gone forward to the attack, giving them double proof of his omniscience. First, as he always did, by reading their hearts, "Why reason ye in your hearts?" Then suddenly, he who appeared to have seen only the sores on that cowering soul, whose gaze went straight to the heart, let his eyes rest upon the crippled body lying at his feet. He turned to the Pharisees:

"Which is easier—to say, 'Thy sins are forgiven thee,' or to say, 'Arise and walk'? But that ye may know that the Son of Man hath power on earth to forgive sins . . . I say to thee, arise, take up thy couch, and go to thy home."

The paralytic rose in the midst of the joyful shouts of the crowd. And no doubt the Pharisees took advantage of the tumult to disappear. But the scribe I have in mind—perhaps the one spoken of by St. Matthew—was carried away, and he cried out to Jesus: "Master, I will follow thee whithersoever thou go."

He was seduced by the seducer; he submitted to omnipotence, gave up his alms. No doubt he awaited a look, a word which would repay him for so prompt a surrender. But what came from the mouth of this man was never what one expected. Jesus, still trembling from what he had accomplished, replied:

"The foxes have holes, and the birds of heaven nests, but the Son of Man hath not where to lay his head."

He seemed to say, "You have long taken me for a seducer—well, here are my allurements, and what I hold out to those who love me. And this renunciation is the kindest part of what I reserve for them. Soon, in this empty place, in this nothingness, I will spread a bed for them where the place for the feet and hands is marked beforehand."

And perhaps the scribe thought, "I was too hasty. . . . He wishes to try me because he does not know me." Now, at that moment, a voice was raised among the disciples who were close to the Master:

"Lord, permit me first to go and bury my father."

"Follow me, and leave the dead to bury their dead."

The dross of centuries covers the hard and piercing metal of these words. Centuries of assuasive commentary, of attenuations. Because the truth is never looked in the face, the literal truth of these words is not accepted. But why! We have means of knowing how true they are if at an official funeral we look about us, at those sick and crafty faces, marked by the double usury of time and crime, that macerated flesh, steeped in vice, the crowd of bodies (and our own among them) whose corruption is more advanced than that of the dead they have come to honour. For of the dead at least only the corpse remains; the soul is elsewhere, purified by an unknown fire. But we who believe ourselves the survivors are the ones who stink: the odour of spiritual decay surpasses the other.

"Leave the dead to bury their dead. . . ." Perhaps the scribe could hear no more. Perhaps the disciple went away. Nevertheless, it is here that Christ spoke as God. If he had cried, "I am God!" he could not have declared himself more clearly. For God alone can we leave to hirelings the care of burying that poor body which gave us birth. Still, this does not prevent me from looking in vain among my neighbours, among all the good families I know, to find a single man or woman whose mind would not be unhinged by this requirement of Christ. Every one of his words gained him souls and sent away others. Around him hearts came and went, in a perpetual flux.

MATTHEW'S VOCATION

And suddenly the Son of God, who had his reasons for disconcerting the scribe and the disciple, stopped on the shore of the lake before the little table where a publican was seated; one of those most reviled and distrusted by the Jews, of the lower order of those pillaging folk appointed by the state to collect certain taxes. They harassed the people and basely committed themselves with the Gentiles; they were the scum of society. Jesus therefore looked at this Levi, son of Alphæus, seated at the place of toll, and said to him, "Follow me!"

No doubt he already knew him, just as Simon and the sons of Zebedee were his friends before he gave them the command to leave all. Passing by, the Master must often have seen a dog-like look cast in his direction. His heart was touched by the desire of a creature filled with love for him but who thought that a publican could not allow himself to address the Son of Man, much less to become one of his followers. Jesus, who hated the complacency of false saints, could not resist in a man that persuasion of his own misery which humbled the creature before the purity of God.

Levi (did he yet call himself Matthew?) therefore rose and followed Jesus. Or rather, to the stupor and the scandal and also to the joy of the Pharisees, re-forming in a group at a distance, it was Jesus who followed the unclean tax collector, entered his house and seated himself at his table where a rabble was gathered—people of Levi's ilk, and those of whom certain people still say, "one should not recognise them," "they are not received." The doctors took their revenge; near the door they surrounded the intimidated disciples and dealt them a direct blow. "Why doth your master eat with publicans and sinners?" And they could find no answer. Then from the midst of the guests, the powerful voice was raised:

"They that are strong have no need of a physician, but they that are infirm. Go and learn (in what a tone he sent back these theologians to their studies!), go ye and learn what this meaneth: 'Mercy I desire, and not sacrifice.' I have come, not to call just men, but sinners."

There is a kind of hypocrisy which is worse than that of the Pharisees: it is to hide behind Christ's example in order to follow one's own lustful desires and to seek out the company of the dissolute. He was a hunter who followed souls to their burrows. He did not seek his pleasure with easy creatures. But as for ourselves they are the cause of our undoing, and we do not save them.

IX

THE PHARISEES could no longer ignore the impossible claims of this man. We must understand the Israelite's conception of the "only God," as a personality separated from his creatures by an unfathomable chasm. Thenceforth their method was to compare with the Scripture texts, with the letter of the Torah, every act of the blasphemer, every word of his that they overheard. If his disciples gathered corn on the Sabbath, or if on that day he himself cured a withered hand, the pack was there in full cry, keeping the score for the day when the account would be settled. But he, far from defending himself, braved them, and with what recklessness!

"*The Son of Man is lord even of the sabbath.*" Who did he think he was? Was he mad? He had already had the temerity to say, "The sabbath was made for man, not man for the sabbath . . ." and that was a bit strong—but lord of the sabbath! From that day forward, his downfall was decided. Nevertheless, he had moments of return to prudence. We may not say that God betrayed himself too quickly, that he changed his course, that sometimes he allowed himself to breathe at the surface when there was no one to see him save a poor woman from Sychar. We might say, however, that in public he still tried to stifle the outbursts which would reveal him as the Author of life. But he had not been able to hold back the declaration that he was lord even of the sabbath.

Already, in many hearts, he was crucified. Secret meetings were even then being held in Jerusalem. There was not a day to be lost, for the time to sow was short. He measured the time left to him. Still but a few months to enlighten the poor people he had decided to use, and who must renew the face of the earth. Doubtless they loved him ardently, and that was the necessary thing. But as yet—they understood nothing.

Save one perhaps, the Man of Kerioth, Judas, the last of the Twelve to be called from among all his disciples. He was chosen after Simon and Andrew, after James and John, Philip and Bartholomew, after Matthew and Thomas, after the other James, son of Alphæus, and the other Simon called the Zealot, and Jude. How was Judas won? He held the purse; he was thus the practical man, who doubtless showed at first the greatest faith in Jesus, since being successful he had followed him, having an indomitable faith in the temporal success of the Lord. The others had this faith also, but in a lesser degree than Judas. Those nearest the heart of Jesus, even the son of Zebedee, believed their fortunes assured. Already they could see the grandeur of the thrones that awaited them.

During those three years, for his own account and on a small scale, Judas was to exploit his position, to handle the profits. Intelligent, but short-sighted, when all was to melt away (by the fault of this fool, he believed, who had squandered his magnificent gifts as he pleased and antagonised everybody), he did not understand that the business—and for him it was a business—was to rebound, and that the result he had expected was to be unimaginably surpassed. And Christ knew this also. Judas was there with him from the beginning, he was there now, and he would be there until the end.

Despite all this, Jesus had never tried to deceive them. "Possess not gold nor silver," he commanded them when sending them forth two by two to bear the good tidings, "nor copper in your girdles; no wallet for the journey, nor two tunics, nor sandals, nor a staff. . . ." Judas smiled and thought, "If one had to take to the letter all that the dear Lord says!"

"Behold, I send you forth as sheep in the midst of wolves." (Judas murmured, "Speak for the others.") "Be ye therefore wise as serpents. . . ." And Judas, "As for that, count on me!"

"Beware ye of men; for they shall . . . scourge you in their synagogues." ("Not I," thought Judas. "I know how to talk to them!") And he scorned his companions as he saw them tremble when the

Master prophesied, "Brother shall deliver up brother to death, and a father his child; and children shall rise up against parents, and shall put them to death." Why this stupefaction? Observing his comrades out of the corner of his eye, Judas wondered what idea they all had of the family. For a long time Judas had known it was true that there were fathers and children who hated each other. He loved in Christ his simple view of things, his divine glance at human depravity. And at that very moment the Master proclaimed, "And ye shall be hated by all because of my name!" Well, yes . . . but Judas was not afraid of this. The others trembled, but he, Judas, was willing to be hated, provided he could be feared. And feared he would be, since he would wield the master-stroke: Jesus' own power over life and over matter. The day when he would be free to drive out devils and to cure the sick, he would mock at the hate or love of a boot-licking world.

"Have no fear," Jesus continued, "of them that kill the body, but cannot kill the soul; but fear ye rather him that can destroy both soul and body in hell." Judas shrugged his shoulders; why should he fear Beelzebub, since he was to have the advantage of him, and they could barter together, power for power? "Since I will be able to drive him out, I will also be able to obtain from him all the kingdoms of the earth. . . ."

And yet . . . even the Man of Kerioth was moved. How was it possible not to love Jesus? In him alone should one trust blindly. The voice of the Master was softened to reassure his poor trembling friends: "Are not two sparrows sold for a penny? And not one of them falleth to the ground without your Father. . . . Wherefore fear ye not; ye are of greater worth than many sparrows. Everyone, therefore, that shall confess me before men, him I also shall confess before my Father who is in the heavens; but he that shall deny me before men, him also I shall deny before my Father."

Judas recovered himself; he was not keen about this appeal to the heart; here he understood less than the others. At the least caress they responded happily, attached to their Master like dogs. And the bursar was irritated at feeling them preferred to himself.

But suddenly Jesus' voice grew deeper: "Think not that I have come to cast peace upon the earth; I have not come to cast peace, but a sword. ("At last!" Judas thought.) For I have come to set man at variance with his father, and a daughter with her mother, and a daughter-in-law with her mother-in-law; and a man's enemies shall be of his own household. He that loveth father or mother more than me is not worthy of me; and he that loveth son or daughter more than me is not worthy of me."

In the mouth of any man these would have been monstrous words. If we did not fear, by too bold an image, to offend against the teaching that God's two natures are one, we would say that here again God raised his powerful head to the surface of humanity, that he emerged from the flesh. Judas believed that he understood these words of hate. . . . In truth it was the others who dimly perceived that they could be uttered only by incarnate love without the speaker being struck by lightning. Judas dreamed of a world conquered by Christ, wherein the elect or chosen would be no longer embarrassed by human sentiments. The triumph of force, a triumphant solitude! Surely for the Man of Kerioth there were things to be taken and things to be left in what the Master said. Now he was speaking of a cross! To hear him one would think that he who followed him without taking up his cross was not worthy of him. Judas smiled: as if it were a question of being worthy of him. He would follow the Lord and leave the cross to others.

These words Judas applied to himself, "He that hath found his life shall lose it; and he that hath lost his life for my sake shall find it." Of course—Judas had renounced all, he had left everything to follow the Lord. He had dropped a business which was not going badly. He had antagonised some important people, at the same time retaining what he could of his hold over them.

And with bitterness he let his thoughts dwell on the fact that eleven others who had done no more than he were more loved than himself.

Then Jesus said again, "He that receiveth you, receiveth me." Judas meditated these most precious words of all, full of magnificent consequences. And here were others that delighted him, "And whosoever shall give one of these little ones but a cup of cold water to drink because he is a disciple, amen I say to you, he shall not lose his reward." Judas thought, "I am still one of these little ones, but I will grow quickly because the cup of cold water will not long remain a cup of cold water."

These same words were received by eleven other hearts which did not as yet understand them, but which, like good soil, received them without their owners being aware of their meaning. They contained the secret of secrets; that is, that love is not a sentiment, a passion, but a person—someone. A man? Yes, a man. God? Yes, God. He who was before them, and who must be preferred to every other—it was not enough to say that he alone must be adored. And evil to him who was scandalised! Those who were "his own" could go through life with their eyes closed, having no longer anything to fear of men. Nothing more to fear, nothing more to expect. They had given everything in order to attain all, so closely identified with their love that those who received them received Love also. These words of Jesus spoken in the hearing of the Twelve carried the germ of the bravery of thousands of martyrs, the joy of those who would suffer for Christ. Thenceforth, and no matter what horrible thing might happen to them, the friends of Jesus had but to lift their eyes to see the open heaven.

X

WHEN he came down the mountain-side with the delighted and trembling Twelve, he stopped halfway on a stretch of level land. Not only did the crowd of disciples bar the way, but a multitude had come from Jerusalem, Tyre and Sidon. He had spoken to his friends in secret. And now he was to deliver to the multitude of men those words for which he had come into the world. There was almost nothing he was to say to his hearers the essence of which was not to be discovered in this or that verse of the Psalms. Before him the prophets had hinted at such things. But he, the Nazarene, spoke as one having authority. *"And I say unto you. . . ."* It was the accent which was new; the smallest word had an incalculable meaning. For another human it would have seemed no more vain to cry, "Let there be light," than to declare, "A new commandment I give to you, that ye love one another." But when it is God who speaks, the light rains down obediently upon the earth, and when Christ preached on earth a spring of love, hitherto unknown, gushed forth in the hard heart of the Roman empire.

"Blessed . . . Blessed . . . Blessed." Those in the back of the crowd, who could hear only this word cried out nine times, might gather that the message was one of good cheer. And they were right. By a transformation more amazing than that of Cana, poverty is changed into riches, and tears into joy. The earth belongs not to the warlike but to the meek.

Only, every beatitude implies a malediction. "Blessed are the poor in spirit, for theirs is the kingdom of the heavens," signifies that those who have not spiritual detachment are banished from the Kingdom. "Blessed are the pure of heart, for they shall see God," leaves it to be understood that the unclean of heart will not see

God. Now these virtues crowned with beatitude are just those most
contrary to nature. For in the final analysis, who is poor in spirit?
Who can pride himself on having admired spiritual poverty in a
man, even a pious man? Among those who believe themselves
perfect, passionate attachment to one's own views is held in
honour.

"Blessed are the meek for they shall inherit the land. . . .
Blessed are the peacemakers, for they shall be called children of
God." The world is harsh. Meekness is still and will always be
looked upon with suspicion. From childhood, in the infant classes,
the meek are persecuted. Nietzsche is fundamentally the philos-
opher of common sense.

Is the modern world less harsh than the ancient world? Nothing
is changed, save that of those beatitudes proclaimed once for all
from the mountain-side, not one will pass away; from generation to
generation some created beings will transmit them from heart
to heart. And this is enough: "Ye are the salt of the earth."

Only a handful of this salt is needed to save the human mass
from corruption. But let this salt not lose its savour! The happiness
which he brought to men, which he announced in this first sermon,
Christ saw menaced at every turn. What did "purity" mean to
these poor listening Jews? To be pure! An inconceivable demand in
the days of Tiberius! "Ye have heard that it was said, 'Thou shalt
not commit adultery.' " Yes, it was the universal law, universally
violated, but its restatement could surprise no one. Now the
Nazarene was to add to the old riddled ordinance a new commandment against which the world still revolts after nineteen hundred
years, to which it objects in vain. Since Jesus spoke only those will
henceforth be able to find God who will accept this yoke. "But
I tell you, that everyone that looketh upon a woman so as to lust
after her, hath already committed adultery with her in his heart."

By these very words crime is established this side of the act; the
stain flows back to the interior, mounts to its source. More than
any curse these words reduced to naught the justice of the
Pharisees. Thenceforth the drama would take place within us,

between our most secret desire and this Son of Man who hides himself in the secret places of the heart. The virtue of the Pharisees, like the vice of courtesans and publicans, was judged by appearances only. For each of us the mystery of salvation is to be played out in shadows to be dispersed by death alone.

A little later, Christ would define his justice, which is, very exactly, what men call injustice. It was still too soon (they had already received their fill!) to tell them the story of the prodigal treated better than his well-behaved elder brother or of those late-comers among the labourers whose wages equalled that of the workers who had laboured since dawn. It was enough for them on that day, to become used to the thought that a man "of good life and habits," if he be full of desire, appetite and vain imaginings, and abandon himself to them in secret, is already condemned. Because what he accomplishes is confused with what he imagines, with what he aspires to. What he commits in his heart is consummated in the sight of God. The penalty of those looks and thoughts, of that lust of the eyes and heart which is gratified without risk, away from human control, is gehenna.

We shall not minimise Christ's message, nor shall we leave it in the shadow of threats. Whether the thought of hell is bearable or not, heaven and earth shall pass away, but not the least word of the Lord: and this one, like all the others, must be received literally: "If thy right eye scandalise thee, pluck it out and cast it from thee; for it is better for thee that one of thy members perish, and thy whole body be not cast into hell. And if thy right hand scandalise thee, cut it off." What was he asking of us? The perfection of God, to the letter. "Ye therefore shall be perfect, even as your heavenly Father is perfect." The devil had promised Adam and Eve that they would become as gods; and the Redeemer demanded that we become like God. But what did he not ask? Charity is not enough, he demands the folly of charity: to hold out the other cheek, to leave the cloak to the thief who has already taken the tunic; to love those who hate us. Was he mad? Yes, in the eyes of men it is a state of madness which Christ asks and will obtain from his loved ones.

He will obtain it because he loves them. This requirement would be intolerable if it did not come from love made flesh. The thought of hell, of which he spoke calmly, without raising his voice, would estrange none of those he drew to himself, because they were reassured by the call of an infinite love. The heart which so loved men expected of everyone the conquest of self, expected abandonment, renunciation of every care, of every fear. What he wished of these peasants was the virtue of improvidence, that they become like sparrows, like the lilies of the field. What does hell matter if God is our Father? He can ask all that He wishes thenceforth. We know where to go. Our Father is in heaven; those who possess this ineffable truth run no risk of paying too dearly for it: "What man of you is there, whose son shall ask of him a loaf, and he will hand him a stone?"

But we do not come to this Father in heaven by the road of enjoyment and self-gratification. Narrow is the gate and strait the way. There must be no hypocritical outbursts; above all things purity of heart, and not mere wailing. "Not everyone that saith to me, 'Lord, Lord . . .' "

One would say that Christ, having bared his heart, suddenly covered it again as though he feared we might abuse it. His reference to hell is tempered by words of burning tenderness, which, fearing to be misunderstood, he has hidden under a thread. False prophets saddened him. He warned his friends against them and gave them a touchstone to judge those men who speak to us in the name of Christ. This touchstone is holiness: "By their fruits ye shall know them." The Lord spoke here as a man who, being God, saw what escapes the human eye. How can a man be judged by his fruits? And who should not then deserve to be cast into the fire? Even if he were striving for holiness. . . . And then are we not elsewhere ordered not to judge? O, difficult law! We must not judge, but neither must we be dupes. The Christian soul is called upon for perpetual balancing. We are not surprised if at this game the simple spirit and the pure of heart become subtle, little by little. Nothing is contradictory in this sermon, and yet each thing in it opposes the other. It is difficult to be a dove, a serpent, a lily, all at the same time. The truth spoken from the mountainside has more shadings than the throat of a bird. It is not contained within certain rigid precepts which we have only to follow to have everything as it should be. It is a life full of snares and perils, where everything is done prudently but in love. Unhappily, is one ever sure of loving and of being loved?

Those who are not doing the will of the Father know that they are not doing the will of the Father; but those who believe they are doing it violate it despite themselves. The pride of certain people very "advanced" in the way of perfection, or who believe themselves to be so, surpasses by for the vanity of the worldly. If someone warns them kindly of this, instead of examining themselves they offer this injury to God, and their pride is swollen by one more meritorious deed. And if upon reflection they decide that justice has been offended in their person, they do not hesitate to commit an act which a pagan would call "vengeance," but which they baptise "reparation."

And here we are dealing with saintly persons, or at least that class of persons who intimate the saints. But where does hypocrisy begin? What human tree is not a bad tree by some of its fruits?

THE CENTURION

The interior law, given by the Son of God to men on the mountain, blossomed wonderfully in the days that followed. His enemies went away for a little while. That love for the Father which overflowed to the neighbour, those two loves which make but one and which Jesus taught to his friends, took on, in the course of his mortal life, a character which it would never know again after Christ had gone. He was the Son of God; but the centurion was his neighbour like every other who came to him. During those three years the Infinite Being became the neighbour of soldiers, of publicans and of courtesans.

This centurion, in the service of Herod Antipas, was not a Jew but favoured the Jews so much that he built them a synagogue with his own money. His servant was ill to the point of death, and he loved him greatly. As for ourselves, we are already favourably disposed towards this centurion for whom the death of a servant would have been a calamity. He himself did not dare to go to Jesus, but sent to him some of his Israelite friends to prevent the Master from humbling himself by crossing his threshold. He charged them with this message which humanity, prostrate before the Lamb of God, will repeat to the end of time, "Lord, trouble not thyself, for I am not worthy that thou shouldst enter under my roof; whence also I did not count myself worthy to come unto thee. Nay, say but the word, and let my servant be healed. For I also am a man under authority, with soldiers under myself; and to this one I say, 'Go,' and he goeth, and to another, 'Come,' and he cometh. . . ."

"Jesus marvelled at him." Christ not only loved men, he also admired them. And what he admires in them is always the same marvel; not amazing virtue nor extraordinary austerity nor great theological knowledge, but a certain state of surrender, of defeat, of annihilation, fruit of that spiritual lucidity which is the grace of graces.

Humility is not attained by an action of the will, since it is perfect on the sole condition of being unknown to the possessor. Striking one's breast is a gesture which costs nothing; and how many prideful lips repeat each morning the words of the centurion, and those of his brother the publican! "O God I thank thee that I am like the publican." Thus prays the Pharisee of to-day.

E

XI

IT WAS at about this time that Jesus went to Nain and gave back to a mother her son she had lost. This widow had not called him, she asked nothing, because he had not yet conquered death. No doubt many were saying of him, "Yes, the paralysed, the possessed . . . as many as you like! But he has never raised anyone from the dead."

This miracle must have done more for the renown of Jesus than all he had accomplished up to this time. Especially did it trouble several among the followers of John the Baptist who remained hostile to the newcomer. Was their master also troubled as he lay in the depths of the prison where Herod had cast him? Did he now hesitate to believe? What could have been his thought in sending two of his followers to Jesus to ask if he was the one to come or if they should look for another? It sometimes happens that we have faith in a man, and then hesitate to believe in him because his conduct no longer seems clear. The disciples of John told their master that the Nazarene ate and drank with courtesans and tax-collectors, that he did not protest against this accusation; rather he was proud of it, and did not allow his followers to fast under pretext that the children of the bride-chamber could not fast while the bridegroom was with them. "As long as they have the bridegroom with them they cannot fast. But the days shall come when the bridegroom shall be taken away from them." These words made John anxious. Was it possible he had been mistaken? What if the voice he had heard had not been the voice of heaven! The Pharisees swore it was by Beelzebub that Jesus wrought his miracles. They accused him of seducing souls, and it was true he had taken away John's best friends. In truth, what would Jesus say of himself? What would he say of himself to those sent by John the Baptist? This deputation was a trial to which the Precursor submitted the Lamb of God. It was impossible for John not to believe in him, but his actions disturbed him—or perhaps powerless to disarm his friends, he secretly prayed, "Lord, do thou thyself enlighten my followers who doubt you, who are scandalised or disconcerted by your way of living. . . ."

Jesus performed many miracles in the presence of the two disciples sent by John. Then he said to them, "Go and report to John what ye have seen and heard: the blind see, the lame walk, lepers are cleansed and the deaf hear, the dead rise, the poor are evangelised; and blessed whosoever shall not be scandalised in me."

After they had departed, Jesus spoke of John the Baptist not as an opponent he had overcome, but as the most mysterious of prophets, because this Precursor was not a part of the Kingdom. "The least in the kingdom of God is greater than he." This great bare tree grew alone in a desert country. Its roots touched the Old Law, and its highest branches barely reached Christ, who spoke of it more with admiration than with love. Nevertheless, Jesus and John had seen each other when they were children, and they had recognised each other. God humbled himself before his last prophet without there having been union between them or a total fusion of hearts; as if they had been separated, out of time and space. John was one who walked before, who could not await the Lamb nor yet retrace his steps. The Precursor could not follow. He burned and was consumed between the two Testaments.

The Son of Man was irritated by the complaints of John's disciples concerning the fast. The Kingdom could be entered through laughter or tears. But the Jews wanted neither tears nor laughter. Still to-day Francis of Assisi's Canticle of the Sun does not disarm those among us who are repelled by St. John of the Cross.

"To what then shall I liken the men of this generation?" Jesus asked. "To what are they like? They are like to children who sit in the market-place and cry one to another, saying, 'We have piped to you and ye have not danced; we have lamented and ye have not wept.' For John the Baptist is come neither eating bread nor drinking wine, and ye say, 'He hath a devil.' The Son of Man is come eating and drinking, and ye say, 'Behold a glutton and a wine-bibber, a friend of publicans and sinners.' "

THE FEAST AT SIMON'S HOUSE

The Son of Man, who was willing to eat and drink with sinners, did not refuse to sit at the table of a Pharisee like Simon, of whom St. Luke alone tells us, and who received the Nazarene with prudent deference. For he was careful not to be too cordial nor to go to great expense, so that later on he might maintain he had received Jesus merely through curiosity. He did not throw himself upon his guest: he was strictly polite, even a little cold.

If, despite this, Jesus seated himself at Simon's table, it was because from the beginning he saw coming towards him the woman with the alabaster vase, one among thousands of others who have prostituted themselves, who have profaned their bodies and their hearts, who have suffered to the point of death for earthly creatures. This woman wanders through the Synoptics and the fourth Gospel with her perfume, her beautiful hair and her tearful face. In St. Luke, she enters the house of the Pharisee. But Matthew and Mark introduce her on the eve of the Passion in the house of another Simon, called the Leper, who lived in Bethany. As for John, he calls her Mary. And some believe she was that Mary Magdalene from whom Jesus cast out seven devils: and others that she was the sister of Lazarus, who was raised to life, and of Martha. What does it really matter? This woman has so haunted hearts that the story told of her actions may possibly have been altered, but the essential remains: the encounter of incarnate purity and incarnate sin, for the consolation of those who struggle ceaselessly against the untiring sea of desire.

Jesus was reclining, his knees drawn up and his bare feet overhanging the divan. The woman who was a sinner came from behind. The defiled woman did not face the Lamb of God . . . "and stood behind at his feet, weeping. And she began to bathe his feet with her tears, and wiped them with her hair; and she kissed his feet and anointed them with ointment."

Simon, seeing this, heaved a sigh of relief: his doubts were settled! If this man were really a prophet, he would have shivered with disgust at the touch of her hands.

Then Jesus said to him, "Simon, I have something to say to thee." "Master," he said, "speak."

"A certain creditor had two debtors; the one owed him five hundred shillings, the other fifty. As they had not wherewith to pay, he forgave both. Which of them, therefore, will love him more?"

Simon replied, "He, I suppose, to whom he forgave more." Jesus said to him, "Thou hast judged rightly." And turning to the woman, he said to Simon, "Thou seest this woman? I came into thy house, and thou didst not pour water upon my feet: but she hath bathed my feet with her tears, and hath wiped them with her hair. Thou gavest me no kiss; but she, from the moment I entered, hath not ceased to kiss my feet. Thou didst not anoint my head with oil; but she hath anointed my feet with ointment. Wherefore I say to thee, her many sins are forgiven, because she hath loved much; but he who is forgiven little loveth little." Then he said to the woman, "Thy sins are forgiven." And they that were at table with him began to say within themselves, "Who is this, that even forgiveth sins?" And Jesus again said to the woman, "Thy faith hath saved thee; go in peace."

"Because she hath loved much" . . . had greatly loved Christ, that goes without saying. But do not these words extend also to what there is of self-forgetfulness, of sacrifice and sorrow in the most sordid passion? Is all lost to God in that mad abandon of one being to another being? Yes, we must believe this: all is lost.

And suddenly words burst forth which were the same as those heard by the paralytic, the most scandalous words the Nazarene had dared to pronounce, four words in which God manifested himself clearly: "Thy sins are forgiven."

The Jews were no longer surprised at miracles. Jesus performed a vast number, and they were used to them. And then one never knew; there were tricks, there was Beelzebub; perhaps they could all be explained. But a simple speech, an unproved statement, upset them more than any miracle. What was a body raised from the dead beside a soul which was born again? This time the Son of Man was indifferent to the hidden thoughts in the hearts of those about him, he had turned entirely toward the poor tearful woman with her empty vase, her flowing hair. He looked at the body collapsed at his feet, the body whose story he knew, that profaned temple where but a moment before the Trinity had taken up its abode.

Nevertheless those hardened in sin should not take advantage of this example. She who had been forgiven the most, loved the most. The love of this penitent was commensurate with her pardoned crimes. But for most of us, it is ingratitude which is the measure of our crimes, and we fall all the lower the higher we have been raised up in mercy. If, however, this woman one evening should surrender again to her desire . . . well, we will see her returning, with a pound of nard, on the eve of the Lord's passion, for a last anointing, for a last pardon.

XII

THE DEVILS OF MARY MAGDALENE

THERE IS ONE THING which inclines us to identify this penitent of the flowing hair with Mary Magdalene: it is that the Gospel always refers to Mary as the woman whom the Lord delivered from seven devils. Now the sinner who entered the room carrying the perfume was not unknown to the Son of Man. He did not need to say to her as to others, "Thy sins are forgiven. . . ." For this forgiveness had already been obtained. The weeping creature was surely she who had been delivered from devils. And this was already in the past. It seems that she had come to that place on the road where the soul, in the light of love, discovers at once the multitude of its crimes and penetrates into their horror, one by one; follows their trace in other souls contaminated and defiled, loses itself in the endless labyrinth of scandal, in the ramifications of responsibility.

We do not know how this woman now possessed by love more strongly than she had been by seven devils had passed from one state to another, for the Gospel is silent on this point. Was the struggle quick or was it long disputed? We would like to know if the Master of all flesh used his divine power to ensnare her—or if on the other hand he left her free and trusted to love which, at his behest, began to flow out across all those ruins, washing away all defilement, covering every shame.

This shame is known to us, and this defilement. The Pharisee mistrusted the kneeling, tearful woman, because in the eyes of the pure she was untouchable. The seven devils of Mary Magdalene were all bound up in one sole devil. There exists but one devil as there exist a thousand, and all the possibilities of evil germinate in lust.

It is not a question here of little weaknesses, of those omissions of which every creature is guilty, of those miseries which afflict men young and old—but of that possession which preys on certain souls: those who, in the absolute sense, are slaves of their body, whose sole reason for existence is but to seek the absolute in the flesh. Those are truly possessed of the seven devils, to which we give the name of seven sins.

First, pride: a prostitute tastes to the point of madness her power over hearts, her licence to make others suffer, to make them jealous, to separate those who love each other. In this sense which is worse—feminine cruelty or male vanity? We have even heard such admissions as the following uttered in the most detached tone, "He died for me. . . ." "She killed herself because of me. . . ."

Murderers! And if all the lustful have not spilled the blood of an adult body, they have all, in an act diverted from its true end, killed souls which might have been born. And they have destroyed others which were already born.

The instinct not to perish alone is one which dominates the carnal. Those who compose that innumerable horde which Christ shows us hurrying and jostling each other upon the broad road to perdition are not united there by chance. They sought and found each other; accomplices in crime, they had need one of the other in order to be lost. Just as the animals were grouped according to their kind, these are herded together according to their vices. Each particular vice holds aloft its banner above the troop of those who have followed it. The day of judgment will find them together, and it will not be necessary to sound the trumpet to call them from the four corners of the world: these sombre battalions are already formed, the dark Angel has but to march them in.

Although the bonds of a common vice unite them to the point of confusion, envy, jealousy, hate, mark out abysses between them. And it is part of their madness to feel victorious only in the torture that they inflict upon each other.

Lesser demons drag themselves along in the wake of this hateful and killing lust. Gluttony, about which we jest, may have been with Mary Magdalene, as with all great sinners, not taste for a passing flavour, but the search for a lasting state of disarmed beatitude. Women who hate alcohol swallow it like a philtre. . . . And suddenly the last guardians of the soul are asleep; one by one the barriers are withdrawn; alcohol, drugs, give over to their followers the keys to the nether kingdom.

The sinner with the flowing hair, since she had been delivered from seven devils, is without doubt Mary Magdalene. And we seek to imagine the miracle of her passage from one world to another. As a matter of fact, there may have been no "scene": what is told of the acts of Christ were as nothing beside what he accomplished within souls. Already the Son of Man lived and acted as the invisible Christ. The drama of Mary Magdalene is played within us or it may well be played there. Our own deliverance, or our own enslavement, aids us in representing to ourselves the deliverance of the woman possessed.

For it was a case of possession: "Mary Magdalene from whom he had cast out seven devils." The prostitute was possessed. Is lust then not a sin like the others? That inability to be cured of which the impure lament, even those attracted by God, that perpetual return to their unclean state, is this not the sign of an extraordinary obsession, an individual obsession and one of the race?

There is a terrifying text of Saint-Cyran in which the heretic shows us, in the same family, an almost uninterrupted succession of the damned—of fathers and sons. This extraordinary man was able to conceive a sort of hereditary damnation without his faith faltering before such horror. Although it is true that the mystery of heredity obliges us to believe in a corresponding mystery of pardon, there are races possessed. The death of a fallen man does not destroy the germ of his fall. And the children of his flesh are also the children of his lust, charged with transmitting this sad flame to those who will issue from them.

To escape from this nightmare we have only to contemplate the penitent soul delivered from seven devils. Mary Magdalene triumphed over the fatality of the flesh. Love being vanquished only by love, she lighted the second fire. As in those days when a creature was her whole life, and the whole world for her centred around one being (for the most commonplace mystery of human love is that formidable depreciation of all the rest, that sinking into insignificance of all that exists outside our passion) now Christ was the object of her madness. Again the world was blotted out, but it was for a man who was God. And even the flesh of this woman was included in this destruction; her old desires were dead. Purity and adoration were joined together and were reconciled in her heart. Mary Magdalene entered into the room where Jesus was at table and went straight to him without looking at the other guests. There was no one but Jesus in the world and she loved Jesus. And now her love had become her God.

She was a penitent. Those who are aware of their powerlessness to persevere nevertheless seek in conversion a source of delight. But in a soul sowed by seven devils, the chaff would destroy the new growth if the earth were not ploughed, worked and turned over with labour and tears.

At this hour of her life, Mary Magdalene must have passed the moment when the creature, already entirely given over to God, sometimes hears the hungry cry of an old passion. Magdalene was dead to those she had foresworn. Nothing would ever separate her again from him she had sought from creature to creature.

Haggard, she followed Jesus everywhere he went, and she never stopped until he, nailed to the gallows, could go forward no longer, could not advance another step save in suffering. Then was Mary Magdalene also still, her object finally attained, motionless against this tree covered with blood, embracing it closely until the body of her God had been taken down and enclosed in the nearby sepulchre. So long as she knew where the sacred body was lying, even though lifeless, nothing was lost to her, because she believed that perhaps he only seemed to be dead. She scarcely left the tomb except long enough to buy perfume. And at dawn she was back again with Salome, with the mother of James. Then only did she awaken, before that empty tomb, before that door opening into emptiness. They had taken away her Lord! She did not know where they had lain him! She sought aid, addressed herself to a gardener, and she did not know that it was he (in accordance with the words of the author of the *Imitation of Christ*, "When thou thinkest thou art far from me, often it is then I am closest to thee").

Every personage who took part in the drama of the Redemption appears as the prototype of many whose replicas we still see in life. Souls struck to the likeness of Mary Magdalene have not ceased to fill the world since her time. Thenceforth the most defiled of beings were to know that they could become the most loved because they had been the most defiled. Mary Magdalene established between that abasement from which Christ has drawn certain of his creatures and the love which they owe him, a proportion which, if accepted, arouses holiness in infamy itself.

Among the unchaste, a courtesan is she of whom it can be said without rash judgment that no shame has held her back, that there exist for her no degrees of abasement. Her vocation was never to refuse anything invented by man in the pursuit of the infinite, in the search for the absolute through the senses. In this she could not change. Mary Magdalene remained faithful to her vocation: she continued to refuse nothing, but to God and no longer to man. She was to take up the same tireless quest but this time in the steps of her Lord and God. Still a foolish virgin, the folly of the cross was substituted for that of the body—given over as before to every excess, on a plan in which every excess was thenceforth permitted, where the conquest of self by self knew no bounds, where there existed no limit to purity or perfection but the purity and perfection of the Father who is in heaven.

PARABLES

No doubt this penitent joined the group of women who ministered to Jesus of their possessions, certain of whom were of better birth than the disciples (Luke mentions Joanna, wife of Chuza, Herod's steward).

On the shores of the lake, surrounded by all those souls he had delivered, Jesus preached the Kingdom of God. He had openly attacked the Pharisees on the mountain. Now he sought the shelter of parables—like Isaac commanded by an angry God to "blind the heart of this people, and make their ears heavy, and shut their eyes." Jesus spoke as if to children, telling them stories. We have far to go in seeking the reason for the parables. God stooped down, seated himself on the ground, placed himself on a level with the humblest, spoke to them of what they knew, of seeds, of chaff amid the wheat, of leaven: he dressed the truth in stories so simple that the learned did not understand them. The Son of Man clothed his doctrine, hid it with the ashes of imagery, because he must not advance his hour, he must not yet be put to death.

Moreover, his disciples and even the Twelve themselves must be prepared. Nothing could keep these stubborn Jews from believing in the temporal victory of their King; so deeply rooted was this conviction that, on the eve of his death the sons of Zebedee were still- clamouring for a throne. Before them Jesus patiently compared the kingdom of God to a seed which multiplied itself and which ripened only with time; to the least of seeds which in the course of time would become a great tree so that the birds might build nests in its branches. Above all he prepared them for the saddest of truths, namely, that there is another Sower, who sows chaff in the field of the Lord; and that the wheat may not be separated from the chaff until the harvest is done. Then the chaff will be burned. I think of the smoke from those grass fires which hangs over the countryside on a summer evening when not a breath is stirring. The chaff was chaff even before its seed had taken root. The seed had already been given to the enemy that he might sow it. Weeds . . . wicked hearts . . .

But the Kingdom of God is also a little leaven mixed in the flour. All the human flour will be raised by grace, unseen but all powerful. Hearts apparently farthest from Christ will be gladdened. It was not a question of a brilliant conquest. Love must be absorbed in the world. Christ still hesitated to reveal to them that he himself would be shrouded in this world until the end of time, and that the Host will be found where humanity is thickest. His parables were at once consoling and awe-inspiring because of a manifest desire on the part of Christ to enlighten the good and blind the wicked. "To you it hath been given to know the mysteries of the Kingdom of God, but to the rest in parables, that seeing they may not see, and hearing they may not understand." Let others ponder over this text; it is perfectly and terribly clear. They are the words of a God who chooses, who separates, who prefers one soul to another—because he is love.

THE TEMPEST IS CALMED

His friends who understood nothing, yet understood that he was love and that they should be filled with confidence, not with terror. They pressed round him like children, like sheep. One day when he wished to pass over to the other side of the lake a tempest arose, and the barque was filling with water. And still Jesus remained in the stern, asleep upon the cushion. They awakened him with their cries, "Master, we are perishing!" Then he arose and commanded the sea to be still, and there came a great calm. Trembling, they gazed upon this man standing before them, the wind in his hair. The object of their fear had been replaced by another, for they did not recognise Jesus. Where was the familiar Master, tender but violent? An unknown God emerged from flesh and blood and they feared him. The power to cure sickness, even to raise the dead, might be given to a great prophet; even they had done this. But to command the winds and the sea, and to be obeyed! "Who then, is this?" the poor men asked. And yet they knew the vibrant voice, now a little irritated, "Where is your faith?" In truth, Christ did not wish his creatures to tremble before his brusque onslaught upon a terrific power. It was more than ephemeral creatures could suffer. And he knew that the Son of Man performed a greater miracle when he calmed a heart whose depths had been touched by passion; for neither the wind nor the sea resisted him, but hearts torn by love, flesh excited by desire, have a mad power of refusal. Then the wind cries, "No!" and buffets the face of a powerless God.

AMONG THE GERASENES

Jesus came to the country of the Gerasenes, or of the Gadarenes, which is over against Galilee, doubtless near the village of Koursi, to-day in ruins. What was the reason for crossing the sea? On this shore dwelt the eternal enemy who no longer tempted him now that he knew him. A naked man possessed by devils came out of the empty tombs, the devil having given him strength to snap the chains with which he had been fettered. He ran towards the Lord and fell at his feet. "What have I to do with thee, Jesus, Son of the most high God? I beg of thee, torment me not." He claimed to call himself "Legion"; that is, innumerable devils who, after the deliverance of the possessed man, obtained leave to enter into swine. And all the herd threw themselves down to the bottom of the lake and were drowned. The frightened swine-herds gave the alarm and the whole population of the Gerasene district begged Jesus to depart from them. Thus the Son of Man inspired not only love or hate, but also fear. This God humbled in the flesh and whom the Pharisees did not recognise, created eddies of excitement about his powerful presence. What do we know of the world of dark angels?

The people of Koursi were afraid of Christ; fear is a low form of faith. These peasants did not seek to know who he was; he was a man who had driven their swine mad. To-day it was the swine . . . what would it be to-morrow if he remained among them? Peasants, they cared more fo 1their livestock than for their souls. But the Son of Man was not angry, and the "dispossessed," who had clothed himself and was now crouching beside the Lord begging to be allowed to stay with him, received the command to remain where he was, to tell of his deliverance, to preach the Kingdom of God to these poor people. Thus this man was the precursor of Paul of

Tarsus; in this unknown man we must venerate the first apostle to the Gentiles.

It must have pained Jesus, accustomed to adoration or to hate, to have so terrified the Gerasenes. They prayed to him, but the object of their prayer was that he might depart from them. Their posterity is more numerous than we might imagine: all those who have received a call, who have seen, have touched, finally who know that the truth is a living person. But they are poor men buried in their business, in their desires; they have a family to support, passions which they are not able to stifle. More than burning fire they fear this love which digs its furrows deep into the flesh, which cuts to the quick. They want to be left with their swine! The cross is folly and it is not their business to behave like angels. Moreover, they are reasonable. This kingdom of God involves a world swarming with devils, and jugglery is distasteful to them.

THE DAUGHTER OF JAIRUS AND
THE HEM OF CHRIST'S GARMENT

Jesus therefore entered the boat to go back across the lake, and when he finally reached the other side, he was happy to see coming toward him the affectionate and familiar multitude. Ah, he would refuse them nothing that they asked, these who had no fear of him, who, on the contrary, crowded in upon him and prevented him from going forward. Then came a president of the synagogue, Jairus, before whom the humbler people drew back. He cast himself at the feet of Jesus, and besought him to come in haste, for his daughter was dying. But the multitude was so great that Jesus could not advance.

Suddenly, in the midst of the human swarm, he felt within himself that the Son of God had just performed a sovereign act. "Who touched me?" All denied it, and Peter said laughingly, "Thou seest the multitude pressing upon thee, and sayest thou, 'Who touched me?'" But the Lord knew that power had gone forth from his flesh. Then a trembling woman came and fell down before him. Suffering for twelve years from an issue of blood, she had borne many things at the hands of the physicians. And without being noticed, she had touched the hem of Jesus' garment. And now she was cured. Jesus looked at her and said, "Thy faith hath healed thee. Go in peace."

At this moment a friend of Jairus came hurrying; it was no use going further, the little girl was dead. The Lord sought Jairus' eye; the day was one of tenderness and miracles. Never had he so loved this people who did not doubt, who pressed round him and kept him from going on, who touched the hem of his garment.

"Fear not, Jairus. Have but faith."

Not fear but faith. Belief in Jesus is at the same time the grace of graces and the virtue of virtues. He who believes is saved. Only, belief in God is a gift of God. What is there more terrifying in the world than this virtue, absolutely necessary for salvation and yet an entirely gratuitous gift? Happy are those who can close their eyes and, with the abandonment of a child, cling to his garment with all their strength.

Jairus and his wife led Jesus into their house. No one followed them, save Peter, James and John. Those who were about the bed interrupted their lamentations only to mock the healer who arrived when all was over. But he said, "The maiden is not dead, but sleepeth." And he called to her, "Maiden, arise!" And the little girl rose up. And Jesus bade them to give her to eat.

XIII

HEROD HAS JOHN THE BAPTIST BEHEADED

AT THE END OF DAYS LIKE THESE the Man-God was exhausted. The hour had come for him to have helpers in his conquest, not yet of the world, but of Israel. He therefore called together the Twelve and gave them his power over unclean spirits and various sicknesses. He did not deliver them over to the demon of solitude, but sent them forth two by two, and upon them he imposed absolute poverty. The only rule judged unreasonable by the generations which followed and which neither a Francis of Assisi nor a Theresa were able to impose in its purest form, is the rule of Christ himself. The apostles were to avoid caravanseries, were to lodge with the families who would receive them; everywhere they must preach the death of the flesh, that it is by the spirit one goes to God and by the body to corruption.

At this time corruption reigned in the country where the Son of Man was carrying on his work. Herod Antipas piled crime on crime. He had desired Herodias, the wife of his brother, whom St. Mark calls Philip and the historian Josephus names Herod. He had known her in Rome, and although she was more than thirty years of age, he had taken her as his wife after repudiating the queen, daughter of Aretas, king of the Nabatæans.

In the midst of the kingdom of God there arose therefore that other city which still exists, where each of us has lived more or less, and to which we constantly return; where wine creates indulgence for every weakness, where scented bodies filled with corruption are enlaced, where the unbridled spirit scintillates, invents, seduces those who are there but defiles, wounds and slays the absent; the kingdom where one may hate, where one may desire, where one may tear another to pieces, where death spreads from heart to heart: the World.

F

In his palace at Machærus, Herod Antipas, criminal though he was, bent his head when John came, emaciated, frightful under his camel's skin, and threw these words in his face, "It is not lawful for thee to have thy brother's wife!" Of himself he would never have put John in prison, and he succumbed only to the pleas of Herodias. Perhaps he did this to place him in safety, for St. Mark tells us that Herod venerated and protected John the Baptist, followed his counsels in many things and heard him gladly.

Nevertheless, the Baptist did not cast his pearls before swine, since he did not speak to him of Christ, as is proved by the emotion of Herod when after John's death, he heard of Jesus' miracles: "John, whom I beheaded—it is he, risen again!"

But the friendship of Herod for his prisoner did not measure up to the hate of Herodias. This blind and crowned slave, who had climbed to power in the days when the Redeemer walked upon earth, this petty king who trembled before Rome but was the master of Galilee, and for whom crime did not exist, had reached the ultimate in slavery. The woman who dominated him desired the head of the saint and awaited her hour.

It was to come in the evening, when pleasure had reached its height, when the flesh was both joyful and excited, when wine had increased tenfold and rendered almost unbearable the happiness of reigning over bodies and minds. Herodias, all powerful, was not afraid to play with this unclean desire. At the end of the banquet, she called to her the child Salome and bade her to dance—this little girl who was the child of her first husband. There were present the officers of the court and all who were of importance in Galilee. "Blessed are the pure in heart"—as yet these words had not had time to take root. Even those in the hall who adored the true God fixed this young reptile with devouring gaze. "Whatsoever thou shalt ask of me, I will give it thee, unto half of my kingdom," cried the Tetrarch at the height of that ecstasy here below—the perfect joy of the flesh. This is what is called living. He lived, he could flatter himself at having known the ultimate in happiness, at the antipode of another Beatitude who lived and breathed only a short distance away in the heart of the Galilean night, in one of those solitary places where the Son of Man had withdrawn to pray.

The little girl went out and asked her mother, "For what am I to ask?" Herodias replied, "For the head of John the Baptist." The child Salome was not in the least surprised nor shocked.

"The king, though much grieved, yet because of his oaths and his guests, was unwilling to slight her. And straightway the king sent an executioner with orders to bring the head. And the man departed and beheaded John in the prison, and brought the head upon a dish and gave it to the maiden, and the maiden gave it to her mother."

And John the Baptist tasted joy at last, and knew the Being before Whom he had trod on earth; and he possessed Him.

XIV

THE DAYS FOLLOWING THIS MURDER were those when the human reputation of Jesus was at its height (to the point that the Tetrarch was anxious), and also the love he inspired; but the hate toward him was greater still. Perhaps we must place at about this time a brief journey he made to Jerusalem for a feast of the Jews which St. John does not mention by name. He seems to have taken this journey in secret, and without the Twelve, whom he had sent out two by two, across Galilee. In the midst of the enemy camp and alone, he did that for which he had come, but with that wisdom of the serpent he had counselled upon his followers.

On the sabbath, under one of the five porches of the sheep-pool, and without raising his voice, he commanded a man paralysed for thirty-eight years, "Arise, take up thy pallet, and walk." And suddenly, as though he had done him an ill turn, the man disappeared into the crowd. As a matter of fact, it was a crime in the eyes of the Jews to persuade a man to carry his pallet on the sabbath day. Inquiries were made, and the man who had been miraculously cured and who in the meantime had met Jesus in the Temple, denounced him.

The Nazarene then turned and faced his enemies. He spoke to the Jews of the relationship between the Son and the Father with such audacity that he was forced to flee the holy city, so as not to hasten the hour of darkness.

MULTIPLICATION OF THE LOAVES

The Twelve awaited him on the shores of the lake; they had returned from their mission, stupefied with what they had accomplished in the name of Jesus. At this time Judas of Kerioth must have felt certain that he was about to attain his ends and that his Master was shortly to deal a decisive blow. It would be lucky then to have been one of his first friends! All were happy, but exhausted. So many people harried them they had not even time to eat. The Master pitied their fatigue and led them into a desert place to rest a little.

Any desert entered by the Son of Man immediately became a human bee-hive. For him no solitude was assured, save in Peter's boat or in that of the sons of Zebedee. Jesus and the Twelve therefore rowed away from the shore. But ever since they had begun to dog his steps the miltitude had discovered the place of his retreat. When Jesus and his disciples disembarked on the other side of the lake, they found a crowd of people who had come by land and who swelled the crowd from the neighbouring towns—a harassed, faithful, confident crowd. And like sheep, all these faces were turned towards him. He was not angry. A human sentiment rose in the heart of God; a divine passion made his pulse beat; for pity, since the Word was made flesh, had become a passion common to Creator and creature. In his own body God has felt the hunger of the poor, their thirst, their exhaustion. He has had a part in their sweat, their tears, their blood.

Then, the Gospel tells us, he began to teach them many things. What Christ said at this time when he took pity on the burdened and bemused multitude is not told us; no doubt because it could not be put in any human language. But we know that none of these thousands of men, women and children were alarmed when the shadows began to lengthen over the countryside. They listened, they abandoned themselves to this mysterious shepherd. He went on speaking until he was interrupted by the whispers of the disciples:

"This is a desert place, and it is now late; dismiss them, that they may depart into the country and villages round about, and buy themselves something to eat."

An irritated weariness betrayed itself in the voice of the Master as he replied, "Do ye give them to eat." Why did they not understand that all this did not matter to him?

Philip said, "Two hundred shillings' worth of loaves is not enough for them, that everyone may receive a little. . . ." There was a young man who had five barley loaves and two fishes. But what was that among so many people? Five thousand people, whom Jesus bade to sit upon the grass. . . . He "therefore took the loaves and when he had given thanks, he distributed them to those reclining, and of the fishes likewise, as much as they would." And they filled twelve baskets with all that was left.

These well-fed sheep were no longer sheep, but impassioned partisans; they wished Jesus to be king. Doubtless this was the moment awaited by the Man of Kerioth, the moment he must not allow to slip by at any price. Alas, always disappointing, the Master took advantage of the dusk to evade this signal opportunity and to withdraw into the mountains, not without having commanded his disciples to embark in the boat and steer for Capharnaum. As for himself, he wished to be alone, upset perhaps by what he had just accomplished and which as a figure of what was to come infinitely surpassed what these poor people imagined. An artist knows something of this irritation, when praise is given his sketches which fall so far short of the master-piece he carries in his heart.

The unimaginable—"unthinkable"—multiplication of that bread which would be his body, of that wine which would be his blood, when would he dare to speak of this if it were not that very day? He had not so many days left to live. . . . The night was coming, the wind was rising, and it carried perhaps the smell of the grass crushed by the multitude pitied by the Son of Man. Jesus thought of his followers, exhausted as they rowed against the wind. He thought he would join them, and he took the shortest way.

JESUS WALKS UPON THE WATER

With a quick step he went forward on the moving waters, without thinking. . . . We know that none of his miracles was involuntary. The Son of God could not forget that being man he should not be walking upon the sea. And yet he seemed to act as a being who believed that he had the right to tread the liquid plain. Foam covered the feet which had been dried by the hair of the fallen woman. And no doubt the moon was out, since far off he saw the rowers struggling against the wind. Mark tells us, "he meant to pass by them." It was when he saw them abandon their oars and rise up, full of anguish, that he understood that they too, his loved ones, like the people of Koursi, were terrified of him. From a distance he called out to them, "It is I, fear not. It is I!" And approaching them he jumped into the boat, and the wind fell and the sea was calm beneath Him it now bore.

This miracle which took place in the secret of the night and was witnessed only by the Twelve, was discovered. For many of the people, having seen the Apostles enter the boat without their Master, came round by the lake to Capharnaum, and were amazed to find Jesus there. From every side came the question, "Rabbi, when camest thou hither?"

They sought him because he had fed them in the desert, and they thought they might again obtain this bread which cost nothing. They were filled with impatience to eat without having to pay for their food. And it was to these that Jesus decided to speak of that bread which was not bread! But the Son of Man, irritated to the point of fury by the Pharisees and priests, became infinite Patience when he had to do with the poor. It was eternal Patience which warned them:

"Work not for the food which perisheth, but for the food which endureth unto everlasting life, which the Son of Man will give you."

In the synagogue at Capharnaum where he had led them, his enemies had mixed with the poor people he had fed the previous day, and murmuring voices were lifted:

"What sign therefore dost thou? . . . What work dost thou?"

No doubt they had been told of the strange multiplication of the loaves and fishes. But even so! They knew that this impostor had more than one trick in his bag. And the rabble was easily deceived.

A true miracle was the rain of manna in the desert. Do as much, you who can multiply loaves! "Our fathers ate the manna in the desert. . . ."

Inwardly Jesus sighed. They admired what was only a figure of what the Son of God was to accomplish. But many would not believe in it. The miracle of miracles is that which does not fall under the senses and is recognised by faith alone. What is there for most men beyond what can be seen and touched? It is a super-human task to persuade them of that which living Love alone can prove. He knew that in the days to come immense hordes of humanity would prostrate themselves before a little Host. Jesus humble and living under this appearance would raise the hearts of multitudes in all the countries of the earth; and beside these future multitudes, what mattered the Jewish mob around him in Jerusalem and Capharnaum? The time was come for the first word concerning the inconceivable mystery.

THE BREAD OF LIFE

"Amen, amen, I say to you, Moses gave you not the bread from heaven, but my Father giveth you the true bread from heaven. For the bread of God is that which cometh down from heaven, and giveth life to the world."

They therefore said to him, "Lord, give us this bread always." He replied:

"I am the bread of life; he that cometh to me shall never hunger, and he that believeth in me shall never thirst."

Christ had gone too far to attempt further to veil the meaning of his words. It was no longer before the woman at Sychar that he unmasked himself, but face to face with his enemies and his friends. Among the latter more than one drew back scandalised by this new aspect of Jesus. This time he had overstepped the bounds, and the cries of the Pharisees found an echo even among the disciples. A murmur of disapproval interrupted him. But he braved them all with his love. He would go on to the end now, and stupefying and monstrous statements fell fast from his lips:

"Murmur not among yourselves. No one can come to me, unless the Father that sent me draw him; and I will raise him up on the last day. . . . Amen, amen, I say to you, he that believeth hath everlasting life. I am the bread of life. Your fathers ate the manna in the desert, and they died; this is the bread come down from heaven, that a man may eat thereof and not die. . . . If any one eat of this bread, he shall live for ever; and the bread which I will give is my flesh, for the life of the world."

The Jews therefore disputed one with another, saying, "How can this man give us his flesh to eat?"

There must have been bursts of laughter. Judas at this moment said to himself, "This time he is rëally lost, and by his own fault. And if there were only himself to consider! But he has dragged us in as well." And over the murmurs of the divided crowd, the same question came again and again, "How can he give us his flesh to eat?"

He himself went on in his divine way, apparently without hearing anything—but he heard everything; without seeing anything—but he lost nothing of that immense ebbing of hearts away from him. Those flames he had taken such pains to light were flickering. And in little short sentences, he went on pouring out to them the absurd and unbearable truth:

"Unless ye eat the flesh of the Son of Man and drink his blood, ye have not life in you. He that eateth my flesh and drinketh my blood hath everlasting life; and I will raise him up on the last day. For my flesh is food indeed, and my blood is drink indeed. He that eateth my flesh and drinketh my blood abideth in me, and I in him. As the living Father hath sent me, and as I live because of the Father, so he that eateth me, he also shall live because of me. This is the bread come down from heaven: not as the fathers ate and died: he that eateth this bread shall live for ever."

The Gospel adds, "These things he said in the synagogue, teaching at Capharnaum. Many therefore of his disciples, having heard, said, 'This is a hard saying; who can listen to it?' "

Several of those who had followed him so far therefore went away. But one of those to whom Jesus had always been an enigma did not join them. The Man of Kerioth withheld his anger. He had been fooled, cheated. But perhaps there was still something to be got out of this man? Even at this moment Judas was in the thoughts of Jesus. "Jesus knew," said St. John, ". . . who he was that should betray him."

The murmuring multitude withdrew. The Son of Man no longer had to fly to the desert to escape the importunate. There was no need to get into the boat. He had gone too far.

His abandonment had begun. In the dark synagogue there remained only twelve disconcerted men who could find nothing to say. He looked at them one after another; and suddenly came this question, tender and sad—also so human; and this time it was God who drew back a little before the Son of the woman:

"Do ye also wish to depart?"

Then Simon Peter, believing that he spoke in the name of all, cried out:

"Lord, to whom shall we go? Thou hast the words of everlasting life."

At first no reply was made to this cry, which should have consoled the abandoned one. Twelve faces were turned toward the sorrowful face. But one of them was enough to obscure all the light which shone on the eleven others. Finally Jesus said, "Have I not chosen you, the Twelve?" And then it was doubtless in a lower voice that he added the crushing words:

"Yet one of you is a devil."

XV

HE THEN HURRIED THEM OFF on a wandering course, either wishing to throw off the track those who sought to put him to death, or else seeking for some hours alone with those eleven uncertain hearts, to labour with them at his leisure. For much remained to be done with them, and the cry of Kephas, "To whom shall we go?" was very far from what the Son of Man had expected of him.

What he expected was to be recognised for what he was. But all of them wavered, hesitated, vacillated—as we all do. Some days, spellbound, full of certainty, they would say among themselves, "This is truly the Son of God!" but sometimes also some of them would think that perhaps all was not false, if not in the accusations of the Pharisees, at least in the reproaches of John's disciples. If they had known where they were drifting, toward what defeat! How could these disciples to whom the words concerning the bread of life had appeared hard, receive even a veiled prophecy regarding the slaves' gibbet where all was to end?

They must be prepared to think without fear of what would be the crown and throne they had dreamed of for their master, and, as for themselves, not to lose heart before the thorns, the scarlet cloak, the two pieces of wood. The little group directed their steps toward the north-west, in the direction of Tyre; from this place they came to Sidon before going down to Decapolis. As they walked, the Master came back again and again to the point of his message: that the kingdom of God is within us, that all the observance of the ablutions, of the washing of plates, of abstinence from unclean food, did not count for salvation. What defiles man does not come from without; he is the maker of his own defilement; it is bred in his heart and is the fruit of his own lust.

On the way the Lord did not refuse to deliver a possessed Syrian girl or to cure a blind man; but he first rebuked the mother of the possessed child, because she was an unbeliever. As for the deaf and dumb man, he thrust his fingers into the man's ears, and put his spittle on his tongue; he did the same for a blind man at Bethsaida (whose astonishing words are reported by the Gospel which still rings with the sound of his amazement: "I see men; I see them as though they were trees, but walking about"). No doubt the Lord wished to teach his disciples the best methods to awake the attention and hope of the sick. And each time he ordered the person miraculously cured to say nothing to anyone so as not uselessly to defy the Jews.

A secret anxiety possessed him; he had an end in mind which he alone knew. Again he journeyed toward the north, dragging the Twelve to pagan lands, to the confines of Israel where his name was unknown. As it was not the hour to proclaim the Kingdom to the Gentiles, the Son of Man fled every occasion to make himself known.

They passed not far from one of the sources of the Jordan; there the god Pan had his sanctuary. Cæsarea Philippi was already near. Jesus of Nazareth journeyed across a countryside filled with groves and water, fit habitation for nymphs and fauns. The great Pan slumbered under the leaves and was not awakened at the approach of the God who would drive him forth from the world.

On the borders of Cæsarea, Jesus finally decided to put to the Twelve the question on which his thoughts had dwelt ever since they had taken the road from Sidon and Tyre. It was to put them to this trial that he had undertaken the journey, far from Capharnaum, into the midst of the Gentiles. No doubt it was evening and still rather far from the town when he dared to ask them, "Whom do men say that I am?"

The confused disciples exchanged glances:

"And they told him, 'John the Baptist; and others, Elias, and others, one of the prophets.' "

"And ye—whom do ye say that I am?"

There were eleven who hesitated for a second, but Peter had already cried out:

"Thou art the Christ."

From this answer spoken there by the roadside, not far from the temple of Pan, the Catholic Church was to spring into being, and it rose up as the Son of Man pronounced these words:

"Blessed art thou, Simon Bar-Jonah, because flesh and blood hath not revealed this to thee, but my Father in the heavens. And I do say to thee, Thou art Peter, and upon this rock I will build my church, and the gates of hell shall not prevail against it. I will give thee the keys of the kingdom of the heavens; and whatsoever thou shalt bind upon earth shall be bound in the heavens, and whatsoever thou shalt loose upon earth shall be loosed in the heavens."

Here at last was the hour to risk this prophecy at which he had hitherto flinched. Since these men of little faith believed nevertheless that he was Christ he would hold up before their eyes the cross toward which they all journeyed unaware. The Lord therefore began to speak to them cautiously, going forward only one step at a time. The anxiety of their gaze, fixed on his lips, increased with each word. What was he saying? He would go for the last time to Jerusalem; he would suffer many things from the elders, the scribes, the high priests; he would be put to death. . . . But he would rise again. Again, what madness was this?

He stopped speaking, and at first no one dared to break the silence. And he, a little out of breath, read each one of these hearts, saw them shift with every wind. Judas alone had understood or thought that he had understood. He could not doubt that the Master was able to foretell the future. That which appeared incredible to the other eleven, he admitted immediately. The carpenter of Nazareth knew what he, the Man of Kerioth, had not doubted since the insane words regarding the flesh that would be food and the blood that would be drink: Jesus would be crushed; the priests would have the last word. No, Judas had never doubted, but how fortunate was he to be sure! He would have to talk with the enemy in Jerusalem. The last words of poor Jesus regarding his resurrection confirmed the judgment of reasonable people and even of his own family. He was "out of his senses" and no one was obliged to remain faithful to a madman.

These were Judas' thoughts as the little troop advanced with lowered heads toward Cæsarea. And suddenly the best of them all, he who had confessed Christ, drew apart from the others, and took the Master aside (perhaps he was delegated by his brethren) and said in a low and rebuking voice:

"God forbid, Lord! Never shall this befall thee."

At Banias (or Paneas, a name coming from Pan), there where Cæsarea Philippi once was, one can still see the thick grass which touches the lower branches of the olive trees. To have the thought of the cross raised for the first time in this happy country horrified Peter, and in the Orient it still turns aside millions of beings for whom a suffering and crucified Christ is still inconceivable. Islam was born of this scandal. Out of love Kephas protested, and his love was confused with his incredulity, "Never, never shall this befall thee. . . ." As if he would have said, "No, my beloved, I do not wish thee to die!"

But at first the Son of God did not seem to understand that these poor Semites were slow to accept something which after nineteen centuries is still held in abomination by the men of their race: a humiliated Christ, scoffed at, vanquished? No, that could not be! Irritated by this reluctance to accept the truth, Jesus cried out:

"Get thee behind me, Satan; thou art a stumbling-block to me, for thou heedest not the things of God, but the things of men."

What else could Peter have thought? He was not God like Jesus, even if Jesus was man like himself. As the Apostle drew back, his head low, the Man of Kerioth thought, "The Master begins to wax violent, he no longer has control of himself."

Then only Jesus grew calm and resolved to prepare the Twelve; much time was needed to instruct them in this mystery. They were not to understand it fully until they had touched his pierced feet and hands, his open side. Jesus suddenly became timid; as yet he dared not mention to them the thing, the object, the sign, the T-shaped gibbet for slaves, which would be worshipped throughout the ages. Since only an allusion had sufficed to arouse Kephas, there by the road on the borders of Cæsarea, the Lord had recourse to a divine stratagem: although he dared not openly hold up this Tree to the gaze of the Twelve, he showed them its shadow covering the whole field of man's life. But a step from the sanctuary consecrated to the cloven-hoofed god, Jesus decided to speak to them of "the cross":

"If anyone will come after me, let him deny himself, and take up his cross, and follow me."

It is not supposition, it is a certainty that such words must have filled a balanced and reasonable man like Judas with a deep sense of security. Yes, his master was mad. . . . But the others dimly perceived a ray of truth; at least they understood there was nothing further for them to understand; that it was enough for them to close their eyes, and throw themselves into this madness. What risk did they run since the Son of Man would return in his glory and would render to every man according to his works? Jesus, nevertheless, added:

"For what shall it profit a man if he gain the whole world and lose his soul?"

Perhaps at that moment Jesus looked at Iscariot who was thinking, "When the world is gained, there is always time to save one's soul. Besides, what is the soul?" Judas recalled the Psalm, "My life hath drawn nigh to hell. . . . Free among the dead, like the slain sleeping in the sepulchres, whom thou rememberest no more." What would it profit us to gain our soul, which is only a breath, a little wind (this was the opinion of the Sadducees)? What would it profit him to gain his soul if he lost the world?

THE TRANSFIGURATION

So Judas thought; even from the others the Lord must have felt a last resistance. From all his disciples he had chosen twelve, and even that was too many. So after six days of consideration he resolved to take three among the Twelve. These he would oblige to believe; he would oblige them to recognise him by his aspect alone as the Son of the Blessed. In advance they would see the Son of Man coming in the glory of his reign, so that in the hour of darkness they might remember that hour and not weaken.

The choice of the Lord was made beforehand: Kephas first, and then John because he loved him and from him he could not bear the least doubt, the least lukewarmness. And James because he was the brother of John and followed him everywhere.

And on this day the Son of God was to shine before the eyes of his three friends, so that one day the beloved disciple might write "That which we have seen with our eyes, that which we beheld, and our hands handled, in regard to the Word of life."

He therefore led them up to a mountain. If it were Thabor, in accordance with a tradition which goes back to St. Cyril of Jerusalem, it was not far from Nazareth. In the time of his hidden life he must often have retired there to be alone with the Father. A little hamlet was perched on the summit, but without trouble he discovered a desert place.

Even though it were day, the sun of his face obscured the heavens, and the snow of his garments wrapped the rest of the world in darkness. A poor Jew clothed in a cloak of coarse wool shone with rays of light. We recognise the description of this from all those who have seen it, from Paul of Tarsus to the little Bernadette Soubirous; the same light as was seen by the blind eyes of old Tobias.

The three men who had cried out in terror when Jesus, walking on the sea, had advanced toward their boat, felt no fear before this shining face. The man who accomplishes the acts of God frightens us. But when God manifests himself, there is no longer place for fear; it is enough to adore and to love. Here was Moses, here was Elias. What could be simpler?

Like the pilgrims on the road to Emmaus, the three disciples felt their hearts burning within them, and their words were almost the same. "Lord, it is good for us to be here," prepared the way for

"Stay with us, for evening approacheth." Peter offered to erect three tents, one for Jesus, one for Moses, another for Elias. Below them the night fog thickened. A voice threw them face down against the earth: "This is my beloved Son . . ."

They remained prostrate on the earth until a man touched their shoulders. Jesus was alone, his face as they saw it every day, and he wore his poor cloak. The usual noises rose up from the plains. But they believed themselves changed for ever. Nevertheless, after his denial, Peter was to recall the light of this face, on that day when the Son of Man, weighed down with chains, turned toward him his ravaged visage. And John was to remember it also at the foot of the cross, his eyes raised toward that drooping head, covered with blood and sweat.

As they came down toward the plain, Jesus warned them to say nothing of this vision until he had risen from the dead. Then without losing time, he took advantage of their increased faith, to speak to them of his death. Again the three disciples were troubled; their minds wandered over the fragments of Scripture which their memories retained:

"Why do the scribes say that Elias must come first?"

As Jesus answered them that Elias had already come, they understood that the Master spoke of John the Baptist when he said:

"They [the scribes] have done to him all they would. Even so is the Son of Man also about to suffer at their hands."

How slow they were to believe! How strong was their nature against grace! Their Jewish nature . . . they loved success, crushing the enemy, heaping coals of fire upon his head. Their faith must be strengthened. Patiently the Lord started his work over from the beginning.

When on the day after the Transfiguration, the main body of the disciples had rejoined them, he found them rather ashamed because they were unable to cure a lunatic. Quickly he warned them, "Because of your little faith . . ." and he added:

G

"If ye had faith as a grain of mustard-seed, ye shall say to this mountain, 'Remove hence thither,' and it shall remove."

Once again he obliged them to look at that which they did not wish to see, confronted them with that from which they recoiled:

"The Son of Man is about to be delivered into the hands of men, and they shall put him to death, and on the third day he shall rise again."

Who would have dared to protest? For they remembered his recent anger against Kephas. But they remained silent, secretly reluctant, and this promise of resurrection did not greatly help them; even the word meant nothing to their minds.

As they came nearer to Capharnaum, their attention was distracted from these sorrowful prophecies and fixed itself upon their childish hopes; they would be great, they would dominate, would triumph. But not all equally. Muffled but jealous disputes broke out, especially when the little troop found itself a bit apart from the Master. Suddenly the impatient and awe-inspiring voice was raised:

"What were ye debating?"

What good was it to lie? All knew that the Lord questioned them as a matter of form and that none of their words had escaped him. Nevertheless, they did not dare to admit that they had debated among themselves in order to know who would be the greatest.

Jesus remained silent until they had entered into their house in Capharnaum (that of Peter, no doubt). Seated around him, they lowered their heads, so that the anger of this lamb, sometimes so furious, might pass. But with an accent of tenderness they did not expect, and which still overcame them after three years, Jesus said:

"If any man would be first, he should be last of all and minister of all."

For the moment he ceased speaking to them of the cross, and showed them only the last place which he assigned to his loved ones. Again these words alone overthrew their dream of power. And as they turned away their baffled faces, their hearts slow to believe, the Lord held out his hand toward one of the little children, who had entered behind the disciples and were now grouped about the Rabbi, and drew him against his knee:

"Unless ye turn again and become like little children, ye shall not enter the kingdom of heaven."

He added:

"Whosoever therefore shall humble himself as *this* little child . . ."

This child he had not called by chance; he had chosen him from among all his companions. Why speak of childhood? Childhood does not exist; there are children. And if it is true that many of them at the very beginning of life are already polluted springs, and impurities are contained in their first thoughts, many others have that transparency, that limpidity over which the holy Face of Christ may lean and be reflected. There was another form of madness which he required of adult beings; namely to find their childhood again, to abandon themselves to weakness that knows no evil —we who have known it and have committed it, and who are tainted. But this is the point: that childhood most loved by God is a life reconquered from all its abominations, virgin ground won step by step against the tide of desire and untiring lust. Childhood is a victory, a conquest of mature years. For however innocent he may have been, the child referred to by Jesus carried potentially in himself all those crimes he would later commit.

"Whosoever receiveth one such little child in my name, receiveth me; and whosoever receiveth me, receiveth, not me, but him who sent me."

John, the boldest because he was the most loved, interrupted him: Anyone then could receive a child in his name, could drive out devils in his name? Yet it was only yesterday that they had rebuked a man who took upon himself to cast out devils in the name of Jesus.

The Lord chided them sharply; he did not wish to be bound by his followers. His grace had need of no one. Even to-day, how

many of his ministers substitute themselves for grace! Meanwhile
the Lord had not loosed his hold on the child and he gazed upon
him so sadly that the little one became frightened and wished to
run away:

"Whosoever shall scandalise one of these little ones that
believe in me, it were better for him if a millstone were hung
around his neck and he were cast into the sea."

Words more consoling than terrifying! Thus an infinite price is
attached to the purity of a little child; his value is inalienable no
matter what may happen to him when he has reached the age of
passion. It is an inexpiable crime to stain this innocent witness
whom we shall all need at the day of judgment—the little child that
we once were.

Here the Son of Man introduces us into the mystery of his
justice. His kingdom, not of this world, is ruled by justice which,
in turn, is not of this world. What, in his code, deserves death, or
rather a life of endless torment, seems lawful in the eyes of the
world or at least is of no importance.

The world! Jesus thought of it at this moment; and he never
thought of it without a permeating indignation. He put the child
aside, and cried out:

"Woe to the world because of scandals! For it must needs be that
scandals come; yet woe to that man through whom the scandal
cometh!"

For centuries the world of scandals has heard, without being disturbed, the imprecations of this Jew, and has laughed at his
threats. It does not fear to be "salted with fire" (this expression was
used by Jesus himself). The world does not believe in this fire
which instead of consuming, preserves the tortured flesh. "The hell
of unquenchable fire" which has terrified so many human beings
since the Son of Man described its horror with an almost intolerable insistence, this furnace where even the worms of the corpse do
not die, does not punish only the felonies of the law-books. It is the
just price of spiritual defilement, of mortal disorder thrown into
the souls of young beings; it is the vengeance for murdered souls.

To a world which corrupts childhood, which deifies desire and satiety, which gives a god's name to every lust, Jesus had the audacity to oppose an almost inhuman value of innocence, to confer an absolute value on chastity, on the integrity of the heart and of the flesh. There is no compromise; it were better to cut off a member which inclines us to evil than to preserve it in the salt boxes of flames, "for with fire shall every man be salted."

Did he see a cruel light shining in the eyes of those Jews, always ready to do justice? He paused to explain. No, it is not for the pure to light a fire on earth in order to consume the unclean. We must not parody the implacability of a God who had fired this hell, but who came to die that we might be delivered from it. Jesus fixed in advance the narrow limits of brotherly correction: first the warning, then the admonition in the presence of two or three. Then if the sinner persists, the Church will treat him as a pagan. How Christ distrusted these hard Jews! He ordered them to forgive not up to seven times, but seventy times seven, and told them the parable of the creditor and the debtor. A king forgave the debt of a servant who owed him ten thousand talents. On going out from the palace, this servant seized and throttled one of his fellow-servants who owed him a hundred shillings and had him cast in jail. The king punished the merciless servant for not having had pity on his debtor as he had had pity on him.

Thus, by an intentional turn, the worse threats of the Lord always ended in words of mercy. Every anathema brought him back to the secret love which he had to hide behind a curtain of flames, fearing that even his own followers would be tempted to abuse it.

XVI

ARID AUTUMN RETURNED, the time for gathering the grapes. And each man watched his harvest from a shack made of boughs (these shacks were also known as "tabernacles"). This feast of tabernacles drew Jesus and the Twelve to Jerusalem. For several weeks, in order to prepare them in a place apart, he had avoided the multitude, and no additions had been made to the little troop. But the Master alone could count those hearts he had called in secret and who had refused themselves to him. Now these filled the houses of Capharnaum, of Chorazin, of Bethsaida, as though Christ had never visited their towns. And all he had accomplished, had been accomplished for nothing. The time he had allotted to them was past; the Son of Man was leaving for Jerusalem and he was never to return, at least in the flesh. That which he had come to save thus would not be saved. The cry of a heart, of the heart which knew that the battle was lost—at least in the measure that God's battle can ever be lost—this cry Jesus was to throw in the face of the cities he had not conquered. He was to withdraw the love with which he had encircled them. What a mystery is the power of the creature to refuse the desire of God! Grace must have suffered a tremendous defeat in these places, for the Son of Man could not contain himself, and he overwhelmed these shores with such a curse that there is not left even a trace of Bethsaida. He from whom nothing was hidden could not recover from this defeat; rousing himself from the sense of depression that had come over him, he pronounced these terrible words:

THE ACCURSED TOWNS

"Woe to thee, Chorazin? Woe to thee! Bethsaida! For if in Tyre and Sidon had been wrought the miracles which have been wrought in you, long ago they would have repented in sackcloth and ashes. Nay, I tell you, it shall be more tolerable for Tyre and Sidon in the day of judgment than for you. And thou, Capharnaum, 'shalt thou be exalted unto heaven?' Down unto hell shalt thou go! For if in Sodom had been wrought the miracles which have been wrought in thee, it would have remained to this day. Nay, I tell you, it shall be more tolerable for the land of Sodom in the day of judgment than for thee."

After this outburst, the Son of Man recovered himself, and turned inwardly toward the mystery of his own being. He did not need to cast off his garment of flesh and blood in order to find refuge in the uncommunicable peace of the Father.

"I thank thee, Father, Lord of heaven and earth, because thou hast hidden these things from the wise and prudent, and hast revealed them unto babes: yea, Father, because so it hath been well-pleasing in thine eyes."

He steeped himself in the knowledge of this indescribable union. He consoled himself. The joy of the Trinity breathed forth in words—words which among many others, the poor men listening to him did not understand. But they were graven in their minds, perhaps because his accent of exultation was heard after curses which had frozen them with terror.

The Son of Man buried himself deep in the abyss of his own peace. He had turned away his gaze from Capharnaum and Chorazin, of which to-day there remain but a few scattered stones. The little troop walked in silence. Some of them were sad, thinking of the fire of hell; what man has not given scandal? And they sought in their lives the names of their forgotten victims. All loved their Bethsaida which had just been cursed. Suddenly more than one felt weary. What good was all this effort if it were to end in eternal fire and the destruction of their earthly fatherland. And then the same voice which only a short time before had trembled with anger, was raised, full of tenderness:

"Come unto me, all ye that labour and are burdened, and I will give you rest."

"Lord, we can bear no longer our own relapses, our own treachery. This is the burden which we can no longer bear."

"Take my yoke upon you and learn of me, for I am meek and humble of heart, and ye shall find rest for your souls; for my yoke is sweet and my burden light."

To those who had been troubled by his imprecations and to whom the Man of Kerioth had whispered, "What useless violence! what foolish anger!" this tender invitation gave a feeling, almost physical, of the mystery of God's humility. Yes, they had tasted the sweetness of his yoke; they were no longer afraid. What did Bethsaida or Chorazin matter to them? Their only country was Christ; they would have no other kingdom than his. He tried in vain to frighten them; his love betrayed itself at every instant: "Come unto me, all ye that labour and are burdened. . . ."

We are always forgetting the family which surrounded Jesus—annoying and importunate, secretly hostile. His kin from Nazareth, who had heard him cry out against ¦the towns around the lake, said to him, "Move hence and go into Judæa . . . for no man doth anything in secret and desireth to be in the mouths of men. If thou dost these things, manifest thyself to the world."

But Jesus did not wish to go to Jerusalem with those of his own blood who did not believe in him, although they hoped to gain some advantage from their kinship and were, like Judas, divided between disbelief and cupidity. They knew that there was danger for the Master in Jerusalem and they did not care, for they themselves risked nothing. Jesus held in horror this hypocritical family, ambitious and craven; and he said to them, "The world cannot hate you; but it hateth me, because I bear witness concerning it that its works are evil. Do ye go up to the feast; I do not yet go up to this feast, for my time is not yet fulfilled."

He therefore let them go, as if he intended to remain behind. But later he started forth. He did not need to make the decision at the time; this last journey was decided from all eternity. "When the time was coming for him to be taken up hence, he set his face steadily to go to Jerusalem." All was arranged day by day, hour by hour. His time was come and he could not have remained an instant longer, nor devoted one more word to the salvation of the accursed towns.

At this last turn in the road of his life on earth, the Son of Man must have preferred to remain alone. As much as he loved them, it must have been oppressive to drag everywhere the eleven disciples who understood nothing of a hint, and the warped and gibbering traitor! If he could have remained alone with John. . . . In truth, the context would seem to prove that the son of Zebedee was with him. As for the others, he sent them in advance, to prepare his way.

Why did he not pass by Sychar on his journey through Samaria? The dry air throughout the whole countryside must have been filled with the smell of must from the wine presses. The days were growing shorter. Did this God, burdened with all man's sorrows, taste also the human melancholy of passing hours? Did not the Son of Man experience, in the mystery of his dual nature, the tender regrets felt by a mortal heart in the rays of a dying autumn sun? Time, the concept of that which lasts, and is exhausted, and finishes, was intoxicating to that Being who later was to brave the Jews with the incredible words, "Before Abraham came to be, I am." But to-day, on the autumn road of Samaria, he was a passer-by who would never return to the town of his birth, a hunted man, already under the shadow of the law; and once more he gazed upon the September sunset and breathed again the winy smell of the last harvest. Yes, he also knew our poor human joy.

But his disciples came back: they never left him for long. Always the same story: the Samaritans did not wish to receive people whose face was set toward Jerusalem. The sons of Zebedee, in whose ears was still resounding the cry of Jesus against the three cities, then proposed with that eternal zeal of the Jew for vengeance and destruction, as the simplest of measures, "Lord, wilt thou that we bid fire fall from heaven and consume them?"

Jesus, who was walking ahead, turned about. Was it possible that

this blow came from John? The disciple was referring to the imprecations of his Lord against Bethsaida. This "son of thunder," as he
was called by Jesus in tender derision, was certainly not a peaceful
soul, and he thought that the time was over for sheepfolds and
beatitudes. Jesus was not angry. In his reply we discern an accent of
unspeakable weariness, of sad and weary complaint, the discourage-
ment of the Divine:

"You know not of what spirit you are!"

And he added:

"The Son of Man came not to destroy souls, but to save. He
came to seek and find that which was lost."

In a vision, fifteen centuries later, he was to say to St. Francis de
Sales, tortured by scruples, "My name is not 'he who damns,' my
name is Jesus." And doubtless if the Son of Zebedee had been bold
enough to protest, "But Lord, only the other day, you spoke of
hell and fire," the Master might have replied, "I am not a God of
logic. There is nothing further from me than all your philosophy.
My heart has its reasons which escape your reason, because I am
Love. Yesterday it was from love that I lit before your eyes that
unquenchable furnace, and to-day that same love tells you that
I have come to save that which was lost." He looked straight ahead
of him; he saw in Jerusalem, among all the loose women of the
city, the guilty wife who on the morrow was to be dragged before
him. She loved a man at this very moment, and this man was not
her husband. They were drunken with desire, and already the
neighbours spied upon them. To this adulterous woman he was not
to speak of hell.

IN JERUSALEM

He entered into the city and hid himself in the house of one of
his followers; perhaps at Bethany in the house of Lazarus. But
several of those who were with him were recognised, for he
was being sought everywhere. The pilgrims asked among themselves, "Where is he?" without daring to express themselves openly
in the matter, so much was he already suspected and hated,

condemned in advance. The affair of the paralytic he had cured on his last visit, under the porch of the Pool of the Three Sheep, was not forgotten. He alluded to it clearly when, in the midst of the feast, he made bold to teach in the Temple (he who had studied in no school) as though he were a doctor in Israel.

No, he was not a doctor; he protested that he had no teaching of his own. What need was there of inventing one? His teaching was his Father's, and his glory was that of his Father. And as his listeners murmured against him, he asked:

"Why seek ye to put me to death?"

They grew indignant? "Thou hast a devil; who seeketh to put thee to death?" The Galileans protested in good faith. But the princes of the priests trembled to hear their purposes unmasked, and dared not put their hands upon him in full light of day. So evident was their fear that the Jews asked among themselves, "Can it really be that the rulers have come to know that this is the Christ?" But no, it was impossible to believe such folly; this man came from Nazareth; they knew his father, his mother; the city was full of his kin and they were the first to laugh and shrug their shoulders.

Nevertheless his voice threw the multitude into a commotion. His voice alone; he no longer performed many miracles. And yet their hearts had never been so troubled. As the time of the Passion approached, the words of the Lord were tinged with a glowing light. "Yet a little while am I with you; and I go to him who sent me. Ye shall seek me, and shall not find me; and where I am, ye cannot come. . . ." They did not understand, and yet they remained hanging on his words. The last day of the feast their minds were more than ever divided by a discourse of which John gives us the theme: "If any man thirst, let him come to me, and let him drink. Whoso believeth in me, as the Scripture saith, 'Out of his belly shall flow rivers of living water.' "

We know to-day that this prophecy has been realised. For those who saw Christ in the days when he was in the flesh, received less grace than we, who assist at the accomplishment of his promises.

Not only the legion of saints, but the least of Christians in the state of grace is a spring of living water, and the world does not know that it is surrounded and bathed in its flood.

With what vigour must he have said these things, for all the people were aroused. "This is truly the prophet! . . . This is the Christ! Nay, is the Christ to come out of Galilee? hath not the Scripture said that it is . . . from Bethlehem?"

But the most astonishing testimony came from the guards sent by the high priests to arrest him, who came back with empty hands.

"Why have ye not brought him?"

They replied:

"Never did man speak as this man speaketh."

The furious priests asked him if they too had been led astray. And not daring to punish them, they reproved them: was there a single Pharisee, a single doctor knowing the law, who had espoused the cause of this impostor? The foolish multitude followed him because they did not know that the Messiah could not have come out of Galilee.

Were the guards convinced? As for the Pharisees, all the attractions of Jesus' words were as nothing against their knowledge of the texts. They were the Scriptural scholars. But even among them was one, who in the secret recesses of his heart, like the humble soldiers, considered that no man had even spoken as this man. Only Nicodemus pushed prudence to the borders of cowardice. He had passed a whole night face to face with Jesus, alone with him, and his heart was still kindled; but he covered this fire with ashes. Nevertheless, on that day he called upon all his courage, and his trembling voice was raised. "Doth our Law judge a man, unless it first give him a hearing?" The high priests faced the suspect, "Are thou also from Galilee? Search and see that no prophet ariseth out of Galilee!"

Nicodemus hung his head and must have returned to his house hugging the walls.

XVII

THIS SAME NIGHT the Son of Man passed on to the Mount of Olives, or perhaps he went down to Bethany. At dawn he came again into the Temple where the people were already gathering. It was then that a group came forward, dragging with them a terrified and tearful woman. Under cover of the night she had been taken in the very act of adultery. Whose idea was it to bring her to the Nazarene? He was the friend of publicans and lost women, as the disciples of John themselves would testify. The law was plain in this matter: in so far as a betrothed woman was concerned (and with even more reason in the case of married women), they should be stoned. It was written; the text was clear. The doctors surrounded him and questioned him avidly, certain of taking him in error, "What therefore dost thou say?"

They were not really interested in the fate of this lamentable creature! They were making use of everything to ruin him whom they hated. It was impossible to predict the blasphemy of the impostor, but they could be sure in advance that he would blaspheme. While they passed around him, crying and expostulating, the unhappy woman remained standing, hardly clothed, her head uncovered. Taut with fear, she gazed with a hunted look at this stranger appointed by the priests to be her judge.

He did not look at her. He stooped down and wrote with his finger on the ground. St. Jerome assures us that he was writing the sins of her accusers. The simple truth is far more beautiful! The Son of Man, knowing that the unhappy woman fainted more with shame than with fear, did not look at her because there are hours in the life of every creature when the greatest charity is not to see them. All of Christ's love for sinners was contained in this hidden look. And the figures he traced on the earth meant nothing more than his will not to raise his eyes toward her poor body.

He therefore waited until the pack had finished their yelping and then he said:

"Let him that is without sin among you throw the first stone at her."

And again he stooped down and wrote on the ground. "But they, when they heard this, went away one by one, beginning with the eldest; and he was left alone, and the woman standing in the midst."

Beginning with the eldest . . . this time he imposed the grace of lucidity upon all. His enemies recognised his power of reading hearts. Within himself each one felt stirring the secret he had hidden from every gaze for years—some habit, some shameful thing. Suppose the Nazarene were suddenly to cry out, "And you, there? you are not going? what then were you doing yesterday, at such an hour, in such a place?"

Jesus, then, was left alone with the woman. After all, he was not her legal judge. Since her accusers had disappeared, she too might have taken the opportunity to escape, and to place herself in safety. Nevertheless she remained there, she who on that very night had given herself over to the delights of the flesh. She had suffered greatly, and had struggled with herself before yielding. And now she no longer thought of her love nor of any person, save of this stranger gazing at her, now that they were alone and she would no longer be humiliated. She looked at him, still full of shame, but it was no longer the same shame. She wept because of the evil she had done. Her desire ended. Suddenly a great calm came over her soul and her flesh, over her desire less easily calmed than the sea of Tiberias! Nothing human was foreign to the Nazarene. But because he was God he knew what no man may know: the unconquerable weakness of the woman, that crawling and cringing creature that she becomes at certain hours, before certain beings. And throughout the ages it was to be the most extraordinary victory of the Son of Man that among legions of holy women he was to substitute his own demands for the demands of their blood. So common, and so wide-spread was this to become, that we are no longer even struck by it.

Over this woman he was master. He questioned her, "Woman, where are they? Hath no one condemned thee?" She replied, "No one, Lord." Jesus said to her, "Neither do I condemn thee; go, henceforth sin no more."

She went away. She would come back; or rather she had no need to come back; they were united from thenceforth and for ever. Thus, under the appearance of tremendous defeat, Christ was securing his recruits from the lower strata. For his secret treasure he was amassing the hearts of the derelict and those cast out by the world. A divining rod was not needed for him to discover in such beings, despite all their visible misery, that spring of suffering and tenderness over which he had power.

THE EQUAL OF THE FATHER

All this was but an episode in the merciless combat in which he now found himself engaged, and which was not to cease until that third hour on the eve of the sabbath when he would draw one last breath from that single wound which was his body. He was no longer careful, but fought alone, his face uncovered (his disciples remaining somewhat withdrawn) in the very city where the enemy reigned supreme. Here he was, among the Pharisees, the priests, where orders were already given for his death, where nothing now stood between the cross and himself save the divine words which struck dumb the soldiers who came to arrest him.

It was not a question of eloquence nor of any human gift. It was a power which no man had possessed before him, of touching the hidden places of the heart, of going straight to the secret of every creature. The four great candelabras lighted on the first evening of the feast of tabernacles in the women's court, burned no longer. In the court of the treasure, Jesus cried out, "I am the Light!" and as the Jews mocked at this witness which he bore concerning himself, he threw in their face the secret of his two natures: "If ye had known me, ye would have known my Father also."

He could no longer open his mouth without committing the crime of making himself equal with God. But the Jews, who knew what they wanted, wished to make him confess this in clear-cut terms. They therefore put to him the question: "Who art thou?" and he answered, "Even that which I have told you from the beginning."

Now that he had unmasked himself, an impatient God facing the onslaught of his creatures, he no longer bothered to speak to them of that horrible throne within touch of his hand: "When ye have lifted up the Son of Man, then ye shall know that I am he.' Still obstinate, the disciples thought of another exaltation than that of the gibbet. What was this kingdom which they would win? What was there behind the half-opened door? The Master repeated, "The truth shall make you free!" And as the Jews protested that they had never been slaves, he reduced them to silence by a state-ment of which every Christian among us knows the truth, and knows it by cruel and hallowed experience: "Amen, I say to you, every one that committeth sin is a slave of sin. . . . If therefore the Son shall make you free, ye shall be free indeed."

This is the secret of his power over so many men. They can doubt, deny, blaspheme; they may flee from him; they know none the less that he alone can make them free. They leave him but to place themselves under another yoke, to turn their grindstone, their own particular grindstone, which is their destiny, and from which no earthly force can ever deliver them, none save that Jesus whom they crucify and love. It is in this, but in a very narrow sense that one may agree with Nietzsche that Christianity is, if not a religion of slaves, at least a religion of freedmen.

In the last days of his life Christ manifested his transcendency so openly, that those who did not recognise him committed a crime in his eyes. "Why do ye not understand my speech?" asked in exasper-ation the Son of God now unmasked before them. And he denounced to them the Liar whose issue they were, that father of lies, the devil. If they had not been of the devil, they would have recognised Christ in those days when his human nature was no longer anything but a transparent shell. The proof of it is that no one could find a reply when he asked them, "Which of you doth convict me of sin?"

No, there was nothing to answer. But like children who pay back an injury, saying, "I am not stupid, it is you who are stupid" . . . they protested, "Do we not say well that thou . . . hast a devil!"

Mixed with this taunting crowd there were many hearts still hesitating but trembling with love, on the very borders of truth. The Lord felt these hearts beat against his own, and suddenly indifferent to so many outrages, he threw in the balance the marvellous promise which achieved the victory over his beloved ones.

"Amen, I say to you, if any one keep my word, he shall never see death."

In one word he crossed again the frontier of mortal nature. Here he was, the Son, divested of his humanity, more naked than his body would be upon the cross, showing himself to the onlookers with divine boldness:

"Abraham your father exulted that he was to see my day; and he saw it, and rejoiced!"

The Jews said to him, "Thou art not yet fifty years old, and hast thou seen Abraham?" Jesus answered them: "Amen, amen, I say to you before Abraham came to be, I am." Then they took up stones to cast at him; but Jesus hid himself, and went forth from the temple.

They did not pursue him. The right to judge and to condemn belonged to the Romans. The Nazarene had not said clearly, "I am the Christ." It would have been necessary for the princes of the priests to put forth this abominable blasphemy as reason to justify his summary execution. They therefore hesitated.

One would have said that the Son of Man had need of their fury. He nursed it as one who feared that the fire would abate. It was not by chance that he had chosen the sabbath day for the cure of the man blind from birth.

H

XVIII

RECOGNISING THE MAN as he walked unaided in the street, the Jews asked one another, "Is not this he that sat and begged?" But the beggar himself told what had happened to him: "The man who is called Jesus made clay and anointed mine eyes, and said to me, 'Go to Siloam and wash.' " To the Pharisees, he repeated the same story: "He smeared clay upon my eyes, and I washed, and I see." Some of them were disturbed by such a marvel despite the sin against the sabbath. One of them questioned the man miraculously cured, "What dost thou say of him?" And the artless beggar answered, "He is a prophet."

Was he going to tell this story to the whole city? The high priests called his parents, who, fearful, attempted to extricate themselves. "We know that this is our son, and that he was born blind. . . . Ask him: he is of age; he will speak for himself." He appeared before them again, and the simplicity of the dove showed in his answers. He held his own before these foxes, protected, like all the weak, by the wings of the Spirit. "Give glory to God," they said, "ourselves know that this man is a sinner." He answered them, "Whether he is a sinner, I know not; one thing I know, that whereas I was blind, I now see." They said to him, "What did he to thee? How did he open thine eyes?" He answered them, "I have told you already and ye did not hear; why would ye again hear? Would ye also become his disciples?"

Since he had remained alone for an instant with the adulteress, the Son of Man had had no respite in his fight against death. And here again was a simple and believing heart, a resting-place where he could linger awhile on his cruel ascent, a humble soul; not that he had need of any one, but he was Love.

The beggar was driven away, and prudently left the city. Suddenly, on the way, he saw the Man. The cured man did not know that he could still be blind and that there is another light than that of the sun. Only, his was a pure heart. Before curing him, the Lord had warned his disciples that it was not because of his sins nor those of his parents that this beggar was blind but that the glory of God might be made manifest. Now there was no one on this part of the road. Jesus asked him.

"Dost thou believe in the Son of Man?"

And the man replied:

"Who is he, Lord, that I may believe in him?"

Simple as he was, he had already guessed. His soul was burning within him, his knees bent, he joined his hands.

"He it is who speaketh with thee."

"I believe, Lord."

"And falling down, he adored him." For several moments only. . . . But it was enough for Love to take heart.

THE GOOD SHEPHERD

Thus he gathered a little flock about him. These sheep of his did not make a good showing. The Man of Kerioth blamed him for this; what was the good of winning over these worthless people? There were not ten men of substance among his disciples. These people would fly at the first attack.

But Jesus said: "My sheep . . . my folk." They knew his voice, and he knew the name of every one of them; the name, also the troubles, the anxieties, the regrets, all the poor beatings of each living heart over which he bent as though his interest came from eternity. It is true that it came from eternity, and that the least of us is cherished with this particular tenderness.

Jesus is the shepherd, he is also the door to the fold. The fold may only be entered through him. Already the Son of Man taught the world which refused him: "Amen, amen, I say to you, I am the door of the sheep. All whosoever have come before me are thieves and robbers: but the sheep have not heard them. I am the door; by me if any man enter, he shall be saved, and shall go in and out, and shall find pasture. The thief cometh not but to steal and kill and destroy; I came that they may have life, and have it abundantly."

Now he scarcely opened his mouth without alluding to his death; "The good shepherd layeth down his life for his sheep," and with one word brushing aside the mountains of Judæa, he opened up an immense perspective: "Other sheep I have, that are not of this fold . . ."

Folds there are wherever there are men; limited enclosures separated from the mass, isolated "pens" in the midst of a hostile world.

XIX

THE GOOD SAMARITAN

THE LORD WENT OUT a little way from Jerusalem, but did not leave Judæa.

He must not go very far away from the city now. But neither must he perish before his hour had come. There were the last day of abandonment and relaxation when he poured out his heart, or told those parables by which humanity still lives. A scribe having asked him, "Who is my neighbour?" he devised that story of a man set on by robbers on the road going down from Jerusalem to Jericho, the road which the Arabs call "the Red Stairs" because of its colours. Was it fiction? It is true that this route was a nest of swindlers. And it rather seemed that as the story progressed the Master was himself present not at the unfolding of an imaginary adventure, but that he, who saw everything, saw these things happening, perhaps at that very moment, only a short distance from the spot where he was surrounded by the "spellbound" little group and where the well-meaning scribe received his word. Here then was the man beaten and wounded by the roadside. A priest passed, then a Levite who did not even turn his head, then the man distrusted by the priests—a Samaritan. The latter bound up the wounds of the traveller, after pouring on them wine and oil, he mounted him upon his own beast, and arrived that evening at an hostel, and left the little money which he had with him; he would bring back more when he passed by again. He had delayed his journey, he had deprived himself of what he had.

BETHANY

How relaxed, how calm was the Son of Man at this moment of his life! At the entrance of this same road which went down to

Jericho, in the village of Bethany, he had a house, a home, some friends: Martha, Mary, their brother Lazarus. Jesus gave himself some respite, not that he had need of compensations; but he allowed himself a little repose, a little tenderness. He stored his strength because of what was coming. A bed, a frugal table, friends who knew that he was God and who loved him in his humanity. . . . He cherished both Martha and Mary, although there was no resemblance between them. Martha busied herself about serving him, whereas Mary, crouched at his feet, listened to his words, and the elder sister became angry at having all the work to do. The Lord said:

"Martha, Martha, thou art anxious and troubled about many things; few are needed—or only one. Yea, Mary hath chosen the good portion, which shall not be taken away from her."

Which is translated by some, no doubt wrongfully, "Do not tire yourself out, one dish is enough." But such is the importance given to the least of his words by those who love him that the doctrine of the Church upon contemplation and action is based on these words. . . . And it is true that the best portion is to love and be loved and to remain listening seated at the feet of the God we love. But it is good also to serve him in his poor, never losing the feeling of his presence. How beautiful is the stratagem of those many souls who at the same time are both Martha and Mary!

It was not necessary for Jesus to be man to love Martha, Mary and Lazarus. But he had to be man to love that in them which was perishable, to attach himself to that in them which was dependent on death. It was still autumn; going away from Bethany he must have shuddered at the thought of what was soon to take place in this house: Lazarus' last sigh of which nothing is known to us: the visitation of death, Christ's fight against it, and his victory. No doubt he already saw these things in his heart, and words of love for the Father burst forth from his lips when, on the way, his disciples suddenly asked him, "Teach us to pray." He raised his eyes to heaven and began, "Our Father . . ."

PATER NOSTER

These simple words which have so changed humanity were pronounced in a low voice, in the midst of a little group, by the man
who had just left the friendly house, on the outskirts of the village.
That God is our Father, that we have a Father in Heaven, that he
exists, this heavenly Father, it takes time in the world to understand. The Jews undoubtedly knew it. But they believed in a
powerful Father, terrible in his vengeances. They misunderstood
him, they did not know who he was. The Lord was to teach them
how he must be spoken to, and that he would grant us all, and that
we must not fear to insist or importune him; for what he asks of us
is the familiarity of a child, the blind confidence of little children
in their father—a father whose kingdom was yet to come, whose
will clashed with that of the creature capable of choosing evil, or
preferring evil. "Thy will be done . . ." *on earth* thenceforth. The
kingdom of justice was to come immediately. Give us our bread,
forgive us our sins, deliver us from the devil . . . from the devil
whose agent Jesus' enemies accused him of being.

The evil ones had joined him again. He was not far from Jerusalem when, by a slight change in the disposition of his listeners, he
knew that the leaven of Pharisees had entered. The day he cast out a
devil from one possessed, the rumour was spread, "It is by
Beelzebub . . . that he casteth out devils." As yesterday in Jerusalem, they accused him of being in the service of the Unclean One,
of Satan, of him whom, in ecstasy, he had seen falling from heaven,
like a lightning-bolt.

THE SIN AGAINST THE SPIRIT

The monotony of this accusation; the eternal little wave of blasphemy against which he could do nothing (what a mystery!) God
as he was, and against which he could make no headway. And
nevertheless it was now but a question of months, of weeks, of
days, and the die would be cast. And the game would be won or
lost. No, it could not be lost; but it would be in the measure that

every free creature holds divine love in check. Did he know this difficulty? Yes, he knew that he was running straight against it, because of the stubborn priests, the foolish scribes with their eye-shades, their harness of literal prescriptions, and all the tinkling cymbals of letter and of law! And they confused the Lamb of God with that Beelzebub whose name meant the "god of flies" or the "god of dung!"

The Son of Man tried to control himself, but he was touched to the quick in the mystery of his being. He replied, at first without violence, "How can Satan cast out Satan? If a kingdom be divided against itself, that kingdom cannot stand."

Despite himself his voice shook, his mouth trembled. Where was the peace of Bethany, the odours of the dinner, and where was Martha busy about the kitchen? Where were the raised eyes and the joined hands of Mary? His fury and his sorrow burst forth suddenly; those who confounded him with Beelzebub had committed the crime of crimes.

"Amen I say to you, all things shall be forgiven the sons of men, sins and whatsoever blasphemies they may utter; but whosoever blasphemeth against the Holy Spirit never hath forgiveness, but is guilty of an everlasting sin."

There is no mystery in the "sin against the Spirit." The text of Mark is clear: Jesus spoke thus "because they said, 'He hath an unclean spirit.' " The reversal of conscience, the affirmation that evil is good—that is the unforgivable crime when it is committed by a man illumined by the light of faith and who, knowing that Evil is someone and that Good also is someone, delights in an equivocal sacrilege. Thus in his own life he imposes on Christ the rôle of a devil, drives him out like a temptation, and in revenge adores the Unclean One, knowingly opening his heart to him and consenting to be showered with his delights.

There exists, therefore, an eternal sin. At this moment, the thoughts of Christ went out to him to whom he had been compared. This offended God appeared perhaps more formidable when he remained cold. The miserable Jews, he thought, speak lightly of

Beelzebub who in Aramaic they call "god of dung"; but if they knew him, they would not smile. And suddenly words escaped him which prudent commentators often glide over, and which were enough to chill with fright his dearest friends—and them especially: "When an unclean spirit is gone forth from a man, he roameth through waterless places, seeking where to rest; and finding not, he saith, 'I will return to my house, whence I came forth.' And coming, he findeth it swept and garnished. Then he goeth and taketh seven other spirits more wicked than himself, and entering they dwell there; and the last state of that man is made worse than the first."

It is sweet to become pure again, to wash out the filth from the stable and to embellish it as if for a wedding feast. But the unclean flock which the cleansed man had driven out, came back, one evening, to breathe against the door; and we hear the snorting from all these snouts. . . .

The women heard these things without understanding them, as they do still, hanging on his lips, enchanted by his voice alone. One of them interrupted to cry out to him, "Blessed is the womb that bore thee, and the breasts that thou didst suck!"

Perhaps she was a Nazarene, and wished to give pleasure to Mary, hidden like herself among the crowd. But this was not an hour of tenderness for Christ, and he replied in a hard voice, "Nay, rather, blessed are they that hear the word of God and keep it!"

To hear this word is nothing, to accept it lovingly, is nothing— to keep it, is all. To keep it against the unclean spirit, one and legion, swarming about. Among the converts of Christ, some feel only horror and disgust for their pardoned crimes; they are cured of them like a leper of his sores. But in others, a breach remains open, as if the love of Christ drew back before certain sores which, only half healed, re-open, and continue to "run."

No one dared to raise his voice again. But the hidden thoughts of these Jews lashed against Christ. At that moment, the Son of Man burst forth at last: this generation sought a sign? It would have it! and it would be the sign of Jonah. This meant that he would remain three days in the earth and that he would rise again. This was incomprehensible for those who listened to him, but he had intended that it be incomprehensible, and he cried out that this generation would be condemned on the day of judgment. The Queen of Sheba would rise against them, and the Ninevites who had done penance.

A Pharisee interrupted him with a honeyed voice: it was the dinner hour, would he not come and eat in his house? Jesus swallowed his anger, and without deigning to reply, followed him, and took his place, not thinking even to wash his hands according to the custom. The Pharisee was astonished, but was careful to say nothing to this furious man. He forgot the Nazarene's power of reading into hearts. The mute astonishment of his host was the last straw, for the Son of Man rose up once more—all the more terrible in this revival of his indignation in that he had stifled it by decorum at this strange table. But this time he would not stop; his reproaches grew into insults, his insults into outrage, his outrage into maledictions. The Son of Man was the son of a Jewess, and it was a vehement and gesticulating Jew who cried, "But woe to you Pharisees, because ye tithe mint and rue and every vegetable, and ye disregard justice and the love of God! These things it behoved you to do, nor yet to omit those others. Woe to you Pharisees, because ye love the first seats in the synagogues and the salutations in the market-places! Woe to you, because ye are like hidden tombs, over which men walk unawares!"

The scandal was at its height. A doctor of the law thought he should recall him to reason, "Master, in speaking thus thou dost insult us also." The Son of Man turned on this new enemy, more detested than the Pharisees, because he was of the doctors, the teachers, who poison the little ones. Jesus detested him the more because he for whom time did not exist, saw in this wretched doctor of Israel the representative of a race which would be stronger than his love. Christ knew that for many centuries he would be powerless against them, and that is why, in his excitement and anger, he who was love cursed the doctor with the sublime imprecation: "Woe to you lawyers also, because ye burden men with burdens hard to carry, and ye will not put one finger to the burdens yourselves. Woe to you, because ye build the tombs of the prophets, and your fathers slew them. . . . Woe to you lawyers, because ye have taken away the key of knowledge; yourselves have not entered, and those entering ye have hindered."

We must understand the dejection of this man who was God and who, at every instant, had before his mind the weight of millions of souls turned aside from the well of living water. And as the cross was already becoming visible on the horizon, as it drew nearer, and he began to have the taste of blood in his mouth, he saw only this gibbet and around him all the crosses, all the stakes for burning, all the bloody apparel of human ferocity.

HE ENCOURAGES HIS DISCIPLES

He went out calmly, in a silence as of the dead, master of himself, for even his violences were measured, regulated by the Father. And so many thousands of men followed him "that they were treading one upon another," says St. Luke. For Jesus spoke with authority; and what many of these poor people thought within themselves he proclaimed at the peril of his life. They followed him fearfully, in dread of the implacable vengeance of those braved by the Son of Man. And humble as they were themselves, they felt this menace looming before them. Jesus called the lawyers assassins, and it is true they did not recoil before murder.

Then, with a voice which anger had broken, he reassured his disciples, the little ones assembled under his wing: "I say to you who are my friends. . . ." Words which must have inflamed each one of these hearts. He told them not to fear those who could kill only the body. They were to have no care of how they should answer when they were questioned in the synagogues; they were to fear neither the magistrates nor the authorities. So little did he resemble the Master whose thundering voice had frightened them a short time before, that one of them dared to

interrupt him to ask, "Master, bid my brother divide the inheritance with me." Jesus replied without irritation that it was not for
him to act as arbiter between them.

He wished at the same time to reassure and to frighten them, to
give them the feeling of uncertainty so that they might remain with
loins girded, with lamp burning, because the bridegroom might
come at any time. And such was his insistence that we understand
how, after the Passion, these poor people came to believe in a
speedy return of the Lord. Nevertheless, he spoke especially of his
sudden coming into the life of each one of us in particular. The
Son of Man will come at the hour we think not. It was to create in
us a state of watchfulness and anxiety.

CHRIST'S IMPATIENCE AND ANGUISH

The instructions of the Lord were interspersed with sighs of
impatience and anguish. Already he was nigh to Golgotha and the
world remained what it had been. When then would these hearts
burst into flame? "I have come to cast fire upon the earth, and what
will I, if it hath already been kindled." The words strongly express
the profound sense of his mission which he had had from the
beginning. At the same time he must have been aware of this dis-
parity: an entire universe to kindle, and he was but two months
from the felon's death. And yet signs were not wanting in this
corner of the world where God had humbled himself to walk
among men, although these imbeciles did not understand. "When
ye see a cloud rise up in the west, straightway ye say, 'There
cometh rain,' and so it befalleth. And when ye see the south wind
blow, ye say, 'There will be heat,' and so it befalleth. Ye
hypocrites, ye can judge of the face of the earth and of the
heavens; how is it that ye cannot judge of this time?"

BRIEF SOJOURN IN JERUSALEM

At about this time he made alone, or nearly alone, a brief visit to
Jerusalem for the Feast of the Dedication which was celebrated in

the winter. Eight days of lights and crowds. The Lord kept himself under cover, beneath Solomon's Porch, and the Jews, in accordance with their usual custom, importuned him to make himself known. "How long dost thou hold our soul in suspense? If thou art the Christ, tell us plainly." And he, prudent as the serpent, played with them; did not his works give testimony concerning him? And they did not believe in him because they were not of his sheep. He cast them aside, openly he resigned himself to the loss of this hardened race. And suddenly, he threw at them this statement: "I and the Father are one."

An avowal enormous in its implications, although it was not the formal declaration heard by the woman of Sychar and the man blind from birth. The Jews, taken aback, picked up stones, but they held them in hesitating hands. So as to give themselves heart, they formulated the accusation, "Being a man, thou makest thyself God." And he, in order to provoke and mock them, quoted a passage of the Law wherein it was written, "Ye are gods." Then this last bravado; "That ye may know and understand that the Father is in me, and I in the Father." The stones began to rain about him. The pack charged upon him, but he had already disappeared.

XX

CHRIST WEEPS OVER JERUSALEM

HE LEFT THE CITY during the night, and took refuge beyond the Jordan where the Twelve awaited him in the region called Peræa, north of the Dead Sea.

Now he was but a few weeks removed from his martyrdom. He remained a few leagues from Jerusalem, where the last measures were being taken against him, where the enemy lay in wait. He was weary, this conqueror hidden beneath the mask of apparent defeat. He continued to protest against the endless scandal of the Pharisees because he had driven out devils on the Sabbath day (again the woman bound for eighteen years!).[1] The city around which he saw wandering wrung from him a cry that had nothing in common with the curses under which the walls of Capharnaum were already crumbling, or the foundations of Bethsaida and Chorazin. In Jerusalem, his royal city, there where the earth would drink his blood after his friends also had drunk of it, in a night of tenderness and agony, he strove to touch, among all the stones of Sion, the hardest of hard stones, the frozen heart of his race; "Jerusalem, Jerusalem! . . ."

If, during those two or three years, he had given way to anathemas against the Jews, a heartbroken cry now silenced them—a cry which, down through the ages and until the end of time would never cease to torment old Israel: "Jerusalem, Jerusalem, thou slayest the prophets and stonest those who are sent unto thee, how often would I have gathered together thy children, as doth a hen her brood under her wings, and ye would not!"

[1] The reference is to a passage from Luke xiii. 16: "And this daughter of Abraham, whom Satan had bound, lo, for eighteen years, was she not to be loosed from this bond on the sabbath day?"—*Translator.*

Thus the sorrowful Christ wandered just outside his tomb, awaiting his hour. He used this time to strengthen the hearts of those he had made fearful. Many were following him whose sins he had washed away. But perhaps he had troubled them by his words concerning the fewness of the elect. "For many are called, but few are chosen" . . . how many reassuring interpretations we allow ourselves to give these words. After they believed themselves saved, the poor people suddenly asked themselves if they truly wore the wedding garment, and if they were not doomed to outer darkness. Those who had been delivered from possession by the devil trembled with fear of the "seven evil spirits" with which the Master threatened them.

PREFERENCE FOR SINNERS

Now that he was on the point of leaving them, Christ reassured them of his love. His desire was that his faithful fear him with unbounded confidence, that they confide in him fearfully, but with loving hearts. "And I aspire in trembling." The Son of Man expects of us mistrust of our own strength, blind abandon to his boundless mercy.

And had he made them so fearful? Then would he tell them plainly something he had already allowed them to perceive, namely: that the sinner is not only loved, he is even preferred; that it was for him who was lost the Word was made flesh. All Jesus' words, during the last weeks of his life, betrayed this preference for simple hearts, capable of excess. He, who was so harsh with the doctors and the Pharisees, allowed himself to unbend with the humble. It was not by humility nor the spirit of sacrifice that he remained in their midst. He preferred them, or rather he hated the world and gave himself to those who were not of the world. Herod, whom he called "that fox," was the only being of whom he spoke with contempt. It was but a game for him to fight the wise men on their own ground: but he cared nothing about reducing the foolish dialecticians to silence! His real joy was to reveal himself to the poor men crushed under their habitual sins and to open under their feet an abyss of mercy and of pardon.

Thus he compared himself to the shepherd of the sheep who abandons ninety-nine to go after the hundredth which is lost; and who brings it back in his arms. In listening to this parable, everyone must have thought, "He is speaking of me . . ." for which one of them had not weighed, with all his fleshly weight, on the sacred shoulders? They had been gathered up, they had been held up and covered with mud, they had been pressed against that breast. "So shall there be joy in heaven over one sinner that repenteth, rather than over ninety-nine just."

THE PRODIGAL SON

Yes, it was so, and they must realise that love was unjust; what the world calls justice was superseded, submerged, by the passion of a God who is not repulsed by our most sordid passions. And one day he told them the parable of the Prodigal. A parable? No, a true story, the story of all the returns to God after the period of folly which is the youth of many men. The son had exacted from his father his share of the inheritance; he gave himself up to riotous living; but he did not exploit his passion prudently; he did not have recourse to that calculation, to those tricks which assure immunity to so many other criminals. His folly led him to become a keeper of swine, to the very privation to which he would have been reduced by the love of God. The swine fought for his own food. Then he thought of his father's house. How wonderful to think that Jesus is near enough to us to have known the impressions of a rich child pampered by the gentle and quiet ease of great houses full of storerooms and servants! He knows the appetising smell of our kitchens, the odour of meats grilled on a fire of vine twigs, the tender respect of old servants born on the property.

It was these things first which brought back the lost son, like all lost children. It was not love, not yet. Still he was received in a delirium of joy, the fatted calf was killed, he was given a ring, a robe. But the elder son, who had remained faithful, received nothing but a rebuke for his jealousy. The injustice of mercy! He who having risked, played and lost, gives himself up to the Father because he no longer has anything, sometimes triumphs over those who are constantly devout, whose accounts are well kept and in order, and who admit no shadow of reproach concerning a single thread of that garment of perfection which they are weaving day by day. The elder son does not realise the pleasure taken by a Father and a God in the laments of the miserable son who is found again: "Father, I have sinned against heaven and before thee: I am no longer worthy to be called thy son." The Lord prefers to all else the surrender of a heart which, having burned all bridges and attained the extreme limits of its misery, and returning in the knowledge of its nothingness— literally reduced to nothing—casts itself on his mercy through the same impulse by which, in accordance with human justice, it would abandon itself to the hands of the executioner.

MAMMON

But these recovered delights are in the spiritual order: the abundance and luxury of the paternal house have only to do with the soul. The Lord has an enemy, money, which he called by the name of its god, Mammon. Money or Himself, we must choose. The idea which the scribes had of riches, as a sign of blessings, as the reward of virtue, was horrible to him. The wicked rich man would go to hell, he who clothed in purple and linen neglected to feed the crumbs from his table to the beggar Lazarus lying at his door; the man who drank and became drunk all his life would be tortured by eternal thirst. What did the division of riches mean to Jesus? Rich or poor, his friends should distrust Mammon, and he would recognise them by this sign. The poor who lived only in the regret and desire for money belonged to Mammon as much as did the rich. Jesus hates money as a weapon used by the enemy to deprive him of his loved ones. For such is the weakness of Christ

I

before the devil; he reigns only over hearts bereft, and those of the avaricious escape him. Mammon makes Christ the eternal wanderer who finds his place everywhere occupied.

Judas hated in Jesus this hate of money, he who already sought compensation in the common purse. As for the others, they thought within themselves, "We have left all to follow him. . . ." But the Son of Man was not pleased with this secret smugness: the slave does not boast of being obliged, after his work is over, to return to his master's service. Like him, even after giving everything they should consider themselves as useless servants.

THE TEN LEPERS

In his wanderings about the city, awaiting his hour, the Son of Man went back tirelessly over the same precepts. He sowed, he would sow until the last day, but nothing as yet had taken root. There were ten lepers at the entrance of a village, on the confines of Samaria, who lifted their voices crying to him, "Jesus, master," as though he were a doctor in Israel. Although they were all cured, and went to show themselves to the priests, one only came back to cast himself at the feet of Christ, the only Samaritan of the band. The Son of Man knew men now. It is true he had known them from all eternity, but he had acquired an earthly knowledge of them, daily, overwhelming. Nothing could irritate him any more, nor astonish him. There was no surprise in his sigh, "Were not the ten made clean? Where are the nine? Hath none been found to return . . . save this stranger?"

THE KINGDOM WITHIN

He no longer became irritated. The Pharisees he dragged after him, like an ox his flies, harassed him in vain. He now suffered everything without raising his voice, repeating to them tirelessly that the kingdom of God would never be that brilliant adventure they expected and which was still the hope of his dearest friends.

It had already come, this kingdom; it was interior, it was within ourselves. It was this renewal of the human person, the re-birth of each human being in particular—this kingdom was the new man.

Yes, surely Christ would have his day. Yes, reassure yourselves, you who wished pageantry, brilliance, glory, all that you will have, poor children! Here the Lord paused; he must take advantage of this occasion to prepare them for the darkness that was coming soon. He said to them, "But first the Son of Man must suffer many things and be rejected by this generation. . . ."

THE RETURN OF JESUS

And, without stopping, in order to evade a too precise inquiry, he hastily returned to that subject which fascinated the Jews, speaking to them of his day, of his sudden coming. This coming was to be as sudden as the deluge on the earth, as the fire upon Sodom—a prophecy which soars and vanishes at certain moments of history, which every catastrophe fulfils in part until the day of its final accomplishment.

And such is the injustice of love: on that day, of two women labouring together at the same task, one shall be saved and the other abandoned. And all of them there were like children who loved to be frightened, curious for precise details, "When shall this be, Lord? Where?" And he, "Where the body shall be, there also shall the vultures be gathered together." The sudden gathering of voracious birds about a corpse gives an idea of that instinct which from the four corners of the world will precipitate the souls of the elect upon the sacrificed but living Lamb.

They tried to understand and were silent, overcome by anguish. Then Jesus opened to them this gate of assistance: prayer. No matter what happened they should pray always and without losing heart, day and night. Such was the mysterious requirement of God —uninterrupted supplication. And here he paused suddenly, as though fearful, terrified by what he saw or what he imagined, as if, at this moment, the opacity of the body hid from the eye of God the events of life. Son of the Father, but buried in time, he put to himself the crushing question, "Yet, shall the Son of Man when he cometh find faith upon the earth?"

A supposition which confounds thought. . . . But each word of the Lord has absolute value. He therefore imagines his return into a world where there would not remain an ounce of faith, where Christ Jesus would be more unknown than he was under the empire of Augustus in the stable of Bethlehem, when his name would recall nothing to any human mind. One generation might suffice for Christ, returning like a thief, to hear these words on every side: "We do not know this man. . . ."

XXI

MARRIAGE

CLOSER AND CLOSER the Pharisees swarmed as they approached Jerusalem, their wasps' nest. With the fixed intention of bringing the Nazarene under the arm of the law and of trapping him into blasphemy, they pretended to ask his opinion on the indissoluble union of man and woman—indissoluble no matter what might happen, in all cases. Despite what Moses had said? Yes, despite Moses' words! "Because of your stubbornness of heart Moses permitted you to put away your wives." Then in the Law there were things to be taken and things to be left? Jesus agreed boldly. He was to impose on the world the indissolubility of a union everywhere violated. Then every generation would be thenceforth a generation of adulterers. The Apostles grumbled, "It is better not to marry!" A terrible law, but Jesus knew that he had just opened a door, had dug a passage from us to him. He knew what he was exacting from his dearest friends—not mutilation of the flesh, but the fixing of their dwelling-place beyond the river of desire which separates the creature from infinite Purity. The Son of Man did not solve all the sad problems of sex. For those who wish to follow him, he did not solve the question, he suppressed it. That the friends of Christ carry their inclinations from birth, that they are subject to the weight of this or that heredity, all this he ignores. He requires that they sit down to meagre fare, that they refuse to slake all thirst outside marriage. Scandal of scandals in the eyes of the pagan, crime against nature, the diminishing of manhood. But as for him, he cared nothing for the approval of the world, "Not for the world do I pray. . . ." The Son of Man knew that it is by purity we go to him, and that the flesh shelters the possibility of delights which, when satisfied, give to the creature the illusion of infinite pleasure

—in other words that the flesh is his rival. He was indignant to see the Apostles harshly rebuff the children who were jostling about him. In them at least, lust was not yet awakened.

Unbelievable demand! To enter the Kingdom one must become a child again, be a little child. "Whosoever shall not receive the kingdom of God like a little child shall never enter it!"

THE RICH YOUNG MAN

Children were not the only ones who caused his heart to beat. With the audacity of youth, a boy interrupted him, saying: "Master, what am I to do to inherit life everlasting?" Jesus, without at first taking thought of him to whom he spoke, replied, "Thou knowest the commandments." He named them. And the young man:

"Master, all these I have kept from my youth."

This was said no doubt in a tone of simplicity, of humility, which touched Christ. Then only he lifted his eyes to him who spoke. "Jesus looked on him and loved him." After looking at him . . . a certain expression touched the Son of Man, the grace of a young person, the light in his eyes which came from the soul. He loved him, therefore, and like a God to whom all are subject, without preparation, almost brutally, he said:

"One thing is lacking to thee: go, sell all thou hast and give to the poor—and thou shalt have treasure in heaven—and come, follow me."

If Jesus had not loved him with a special love, no doubt he would have granted this young man the strength to leave all, as others had done. He would have submitted him to all-powerful grace. But love does not wish to obtain anything from him who is loved, unless it be freely given. He loved this stranger too much to capture him by force. From him the Son of Man hoped for a spontaneous movement of the heart. "But his face fell at the saying, and he departed grieved, for he had great possessions."

He was swallowed up in the crowd and with his eyes Jesus followed him far beyond space, into the depths of time, from misery to misery. For those whom Christ calls and who turn away, fall, lift themselves up, drag themselves about with eyes full of heavenly light, but with their garments stained, their hands torn and bleeding.

The sorrow which Jesus felt betrayed itself in the vehemence of curses against the rich, which fell almost immediately from his lips: "With what difficulty shall they that have riches enter the kingdom of God . . . easier for a camel to pass through the eye of a needle."

Who, then, can be saved? Torturing thought for the saints themselves. His friends' sadness touched Jesus. Because he was the Son of God, the author of life, he was going to destroy with one word all that he had said (perhaps also he saw in spirit that final moment when the young being who was turning away would come back to him of his own accord). "With men it is impossible . . . all things are possible with God. . . ." Even to save as many rich men as he pleased to save, even to bring back those creatures who have fallen the lowest, to take them by force, to gather to himself a soul, still begrimed, from the lips of a dying man. All things are possible with God; this is as literally true as all the other words of the Lord. All! He had already said, "I will draw all men to myself!" O, divine and hidden stratagem of that mercy which knows no control nor bounds! All things are possible with God.

Jesus' severity frightened the Apostles, but his indulgence made them jealous. What now? Then all the world would be saved? And we? Peter murmured:

"Behold, we have left all things and have followed thee."

Incarnate Love covered them with a glance that reached beyond them and saw, throughout the ages, the innumerable multitude of consecrated and crucified souls:

"Amen I say to you, no one hath left home, or brothers, or sisters, or mother, or father, or children, or lands, for my sake and for the sake of the gospel, but shall receive a hundred-fold now in this time, houses, and brothers, and sisters, and mothers, and children, and lands—together with persecutions—and in the world to come life everlasting."

THE LABOURERS IN THE VINEYARD

They listened to him with a smugness that irritated him. They seemed to believe that everything was due them. The Author of life owes nothing to his creatures. When love reigns there are no longer literal rights. How could he make them understand? They would accept a story in better spirit than a naked precept. Jesus therefore began:

"The kingdom of the heavens is like to a householder, who went out early in the morning to hire labourers for his vineyard. . . ."

But why should we tell again the story of the late comers among the labourers, a story which has scandalised the world ever since the hour of its first telling? The wage is the same for those who have laboured since dawn as it is for those hired in the middle and at the end of the day. Shall we seek the reason? God has no reasons to give us. He takes away nothing from those who have borne the burden of the day and the heat. If he loads the late comers with favours, he is judge of their love. But even if they bear him no love, if he loves them, if he prefers them, if they correspond to Christ's mysterious idea of human charm, what have we to say? He will transfuse into them in kingly fashion all the love which they lack. Have we ourselves, created in the divine image, ever been able to rule the movements of our own hearts?

XXII

THE RAISING OF LAZARUS

IT WAS WITH ANXIETY the Twelve saw their Master draw near to Jerusalem, although they were filled with a vague and tenacious hope. Jesus had an object, of which they did not know, a last act to perform. The little troop, still taking refuge in the land of Herod, was joined by a messenger sent from Bethany. "Lazarus . . . he whom thou lovest is sick." The Lord, apparently indifferent, lingered on two days, and the Apostles supposed that it was for the sake of prudence. So that when Jesus, after the second day, spoke of going into Judæa, they did not hide their fright nor discomfiture. "Rabbi, the Jews but now were seeking to stone thee; and goest thou thither again?" He did not listen to them, but said, "Lazarus our friend sleepeth; but I go that I may awake him." And as the disciples, at once simple and astute, shook their heads and reassured one another, "If he sleepeth, he will recover . . ." (with the idea in the back of their minds of staying in a safe place), he said:

"Lazarus is dead: and for your sake I rejoice I was not there. . . . But let us go to him."

Peter must have been absent (which would explain the silence of the Synoptic Gospels concerning Lazarus), since it was Thomas, called Didymus, who took his place on this occasion and who encouraged the fearful, "Let us also go, that we may die with him."

"When therefore Jesus came, he found that Lazarus had already been four days in the tomb. Now Bethany was nigh unto Jerusalem, about fifteen furlongs away. And many of the Jews had come to Martha and Mary, to condole with them about their brother. Martha, therefore, when she heard that Jesus was coming, went to meet him: but Mary sat in the house. Martha therefore said to Jesus, 'Lord, hadst thou been here, my brother had not died: and even now I know that whatsoever thou shalt ask of God, God will give thee.' Jesus saith to her, 'Thy brother shall rise again.' Martha saith to him, 'I know that he shall rise again at the resurrection, on the last day.' Jesus said to her, 'I am the resurrection and the life; he that believeth in me, even if he die, shall live, and whosoever liveth and believeth in me, he shall never die. Believest thou this?' She saith to him, 'Yea, Lord, I have believed that thou art the Christ, the Son of God, that cometh into the world.' And when she had said this, she went away and called Mary, her sister, saying secretly, 'The Master is here, and calleth thee.' And she upon hearing it ariseth quickly, and went to him. Now Jesus had not yet come to the village, but was still in the place where Martha had met him. The Jews, therefore, who were with her in the house and were condoling with her, seeing Mary arise quickly and go out, followed her, thinking that she was going to the tomb to weep there. When Mary therefore came where was Jesus and saw him, she fell at his feet, saying to him, 'Lord, hadst thou been here, my brother had not died?' Jesus therefore, when he saw her weeping, groaned in spirit and troubled himself, and said, 'Where have ye laid him?' They said to him, 'Lord, come and see.' Jesus wept. The Jews therefore said, 'Behold how he loved him.' "

Why did he weep, he who should have laughed with joy for the happiness, unimaginable to any creature, of snatching a beloved friend from the jaws of death? He wept for Lazarus at the very instant when Lazarus was about to rise erect and come towards him with little steps, jumping perhaps, his hands and feet still bound with bandages, his face wrapped about with the shroud. It is true that he came out of the darkness to see the Son of Man enter it in his turn. But why these tears, since Jesus too was to escape from the tomb, from time and from space, and since Lazarus was already in his bosom for eternity?

No other reason for these tears than the "come and see" of the Jews, and especially the brutal words, "Already he stinketh; for he hath been dead four days. . . ." The smell of this corrupted flesh drew tears from him whose body would not know corruption. For it was in vain that the Son of Man called his friend Lazarus back to life; he knew that in the end the worms would conquer, and that they had only to await the return of him who had been raised to life. Sooner or later this body would again begin to stink. No force in the world could save it from decay. We believe with all our souls in the resurrection of the flesh; but every man must abide by this call to decay. If it is difficult to admit it for ourselves, how much more difficult to do so for those creatures whose grace, freshness and strength are dear to us? Is that which will rise again the human flower lighted by the eye, coloured and kindled by the blood? Yes, it will be the same, but no longer ephemeral, and thereby not the same. The Son of Man wept over that blighted fruit—over the bodies of all the living.

JESUS' DEATH IS DECIDED

Many of the Jews believed in him, but others went to tell the priests what he had done, and immediately they assembled in council. The more marvellous the miracle, the more formidable the impostor seemed to them, and more determined they became to destroy him. For, having such powers, the Nazarene could only seek the supreme power, and thus draw upon Jerusalem the vengeance of Rome. Pilate did not like the Jews, and he ruled with a heavy hand. Here were no longer theologians irritated by the blasphemies of a false Messiah, but politicians, people who looked ahead and took precautions. Caiaphas, the high priest, a prophet without knowing it, put forward the opinion that it was necessary for one man to die that the whole nation might not perish.

The Lord, who had means of information in the Council (Nicodemus perhaps), warned of the danger, was now but a hunted man hiding in the outskirts of the city. Ephrem, to the north-east of Jerusalem, served as his retreat. But the Passover was near, and a prophet could not neglect to go up to the temple. His enemies had but to bide their time. For if Jesus had means of information among the members of the Council, the high priests had their man among the Twelve. This man could only have been further irritated by the resurrection of Lazarus, irritated against the incorrigible twaddler who had such power over material things and who used it only for his own undoing and that of his followers. There was no excuse for his failure. The Man of Kerioth still did not know just how at the last moment he would get out of the scrape. But there was no hurry; Jesus was walking into the trap.

He came out of his hiding-place and started along the road to Jericho, alone; and behind him came the Twelve and an exalted little group who discussed the chances of the undertaking with bated breath. Still they understood nothing! When would their eyes be opened? This time Christ did not prepare them, but quickly drew back the veil, "Behold we are going up to Jerusalem, and the Son of Man shall be delivered to the high priests and scribes, and they shall condemn him to death, and shall deliver him up to the gentiles to be mocked and scourged and crucified; and on the third day he shall rise again."

Did he expect protests? Kephas, who remembered having been called Satan, was afraid to speak. Also, perhaps they felt less anxious; he who had raised Lazarus was Master of life. What had they to fear? His words did not always seem clear to them: scourging? crucifixion? figures of speech no doubt. In any case it would only take three days for him to enter into his glory, and he would not go alone. St. Luke says clearly, "Because he was nigh to Jerusalem, and they thought that the kingdom of God was about to appear forthwith."

REQUEST OF THE SONS OF ZEBEDEE

Yes, his friends would share his triumph, and the closest would come first. It was annoying that there were twelve of them. As much as they loved each other, each wished to assure himself the first place in the kingdom to come. The sons of Zebedee schemed among themselves. John must have whispered to James, "After all, he prefers me to Kephas; and thou art my brother. . . ." And James, "Ask him that each one of us have a throne beside him." But John, "No, I dare not." Then their mother, Salome, must have taken a hand, "Well, I dare ask him!" One can almost hear their whisperings: now the ambitious mother separates herself from the rest of the group.

She kneels at the feet of the Master, "What wilt thou?" he asks. She replies, "Command that these my two sons sit one on thy right hand and one on thy left in thy kingdom."

A little while before the Son of Man might have rebuked the three irritably! But the time for denunciation was passed. There were not many hours to be lost. No matter what they did, the Lord would treat his friends until the end with a tenderness that not even Judas could shake. He now sighed, like a man who is to be executed on the morrow, and said with loving pity (looking especially at him who was nearest his heart):

"Can ye drink of the cup whereof I am about to drink?"

They did not know what this chalice was. But with one voice and with all their strength, with a violence which had caused the Lord to call them "sons of thunder," the sons of Zebedee replied, "We can."

"Of my cup indeed ye shall drink."

There were many ways of drinking it. The martyrdom which James was to suffer, toward the year 44, was one. But there are other ways of suffering. We do not know what this chalice was for John, but only that he drank of it, with long and mighty draughts.

Nevertheless, through them the Master was addressing all the others, in clear language, for now every word must reach home. When would they understand that his friends should try to shun the first place, following the example of the Son of Man, who came not to be served, but to serve? That supreme sacrifice which he had come to make, which but shortly before Caiaphas had charged him in the midst of the Council, that sacrifice he now made known: "The Son of Man hath come . . . to give his life a ransom for many."

ENTRY INTO JERICHO
THE CURE OF BARTIMÆUS

What did he wish to say? They were now come to the outskirts of Jericho, Herod's city of pleasure, irrigated by waters from the mountains. An enormous crowd pressed around him. The blind Bartimæus, hearing the tumult, asked who it was, and when they told him that Jesus was passing he rushed out crying, "Son of David, have pity on me!" And as they tried to make him hold his peace, he cried out all the more. "Call him," said Jesus. They called him saying, "Be of good heart; arise, he calleth thee." Bartimæus, casting off his cloak, leaped up and came toward him. "What wilt thou that I do for thee?" "Rabboni, that I may see." Jesus said to him, "Go, thy faith hath healed thee."

ZACCHÆUS

One would have said that in the end the Son of Man showered on every comer, in order to spend it before his death, the treasury of graces he had brought into the world. After this cure, the crowd became such that one of the leading publicans, Zacchæus, a very rich man, small in stature, had to climb up a sycamore tree in order to see him. Jesus knew the heart of this despised creature. He looked up and said, "Zacchæus, make haste to come down, for to-day I must abide in thy house." Zacchæus came down with haste and joyfully led him in. . . . For three years now his enemies had accused him of associating with sinners. Until the end he would delight in those who preferred him to their defilement.

XXIII

ONE LAST REST before the darkness fell, once again a little human warmth. Jesus, overcome with fatigue, was not to go directly from Jericho to Jerusalem. He needed to look once more on friendly faces, on that of Lazarus who had forgotten the shore of death whence Christ had drawn him back. Martha's busy ways, far from irritating him, were now no less sweet perhaps than the contemplation of Mary; for those who are about to die love to be soothed and loaded with humble attentions. It was the sixth day before the Passover.

A leper he had cured, called Simon, asked him to dine with Lazarus and the two sisters. Martha, as usual, waited upon them.

Was this Mary who entered the room with a pound of perfume of nard the same woman as that sinner who washed his feet with tears? Was this contemplative also the repentant sinner? However it may have been, Mary had attained that degree of love which revealed to her his own distress, and the utmost she could do now was humbly to imitate the gesture of the courtesan. She therefore entered as the other had done, with a vase of perfume.

A feverish atmosphere reigned about the man who, having raised Lazarus, was going at the head of the people to force the gates of Jerusalem, to defy the high priests and even the Romans themselves. With many of them hope was greater than fear, especially as the enemy was hesitating: it was impossible to seize the Nazarene during the feast without arousing the people. The Council had detailed several observers to be near him. The Man of Kerioth showed them consideration, but with a certain reserve; up to the last moment no one could tell what the outcome would be.

He therefore remained prudently on the watch, waiting to profit by the turn of events, and secretly amassing a little hoard taken from the common purse—that much he would have, at least.

Only one heart, warmed by love, saw in this reclining man, in this Jesus, a creature at the end of his course, a winded stag, who to-morrow would be the prey of the dogs. For many weeks now he had been going about the city, wandering from hiding-place to hiding-place. The lamp had no more oil (the lamp of his body). All that remained to Jesus was the strength to bear and to suffer. One can imagine the look which passed between this holy woman and the Son of Man. The others saw nothing. But as the alabaster vase was broken and its perfume spilled forth, he knew that Mary understood. And like the sinner from Magdala, Mary humbly wiped the adored feet.

And suddenly the two trembled, for Judas' voice was raised and they heard these words: "This ointment could have been sold for more than three hundred shillings and given to the poor." Under his gaze Jesus held those two souls, one consumed by love, the other by avarice and hate. He never spoke to Judas except with grave kindness, as though he were intimidated by the horror of his destiny:

"Let her be; why do ye trouble her? She hath wrought a good work upon me. For the poor ye had with you always, and whensoever ye will ye can do good to them; but me ye have not always. What she could, she hath done; she hath anointed my body beforehand for burial. Amen I say to you, wheresoever the gospel is preached throughout the world, that also which she hath done shall be told for a memorial of her."

Was he speaking of his own burial? Judas drew nearer to the scribes who were looking on. . . . He had heard only that one word: burial. He saw nothing beyond what was to happen immediately. That sudden light on the centuries to come, "Wheresoever the gospel is preached throughout the world . . ." did not cast its gleam into that dark heart. He too, perhaps, was struck by those signs of weariness and wear which Jesus showed—a finished man.

And there he was still, demanding manifestations of idolatry like this, from women who licked his feet!

Evening had come. A crowd was gathering in Bethany, coming from Jerusalem, to see Jesus and Lazarus. At that very hour the princes of the priests, assembled in council, sought the means to destroy them both. From St. John we know that the Lord spent this last night in Bethany, doubtless in the house of the two sisters and the brother. The disciples were busy with all those humble but excited people who were preparing to welcome the Rabbi, for the entrance into Jerusalem was fixed for the morrow. As for himself, he watched between those three hearts. John seems to have been there also (the only one of the evangelists who appears to have known Lazarus). Perhaps even Martha was quiet that night, there at the feet of the Master. Perhaps Jesus spoke of this to Mary showing her this humble sister, "She too has the better portion, which is to serve the poor (the poor are myself) without ever losing the feeling of my presence." On the shore of this ocean of suffering the Son of God accepted, through humility, the comfort of being loved by those he loved. All the same he knew this happiness of which he had no need, he who received nothing except from the Father. The house was filled with the odour of nard. No doubt Martha carefully gathered up the fragments of the alabaster vase, and kept them in the folds of her robe. Seeing these faithful eyes open and raised towards him, did Jesus think of the heavy eyelids of his three dearest friends, during that night of watching, now near at hand?

THE PALMS

At dawn they must have begged him, "Above all do not pass any night in the city, come and hide yourself here in the evening." The crowd was battering at the door. They had brought him a young ass. He mounted the beast and went forward amid the sharp cries of the children and the women. Palms waved in their hands. Here was then the day dreamed of by the Man of Kerioth! He had believed that the Master, at the head of an

K

armed and enthusiastic people, would make the Romans tremble before his omnipotence. . . . And this hope had ended in the derisory triumph of an emaciated Rabbi, already in the shadow of the gibbet, an outlaw who went head first into the trap, surrounded by the imbecile populace. They could cast their robes beneath the ass's feet and acclaim the Nazarene as the Son of David and the King of Israel; every one of their hosannas added a thorn to his crown, a point to the thongs of the whips which would scourge him.

The Pharisees protested, "Are you not ashamed? Rebuke thy disciples." Then the poor conqueror, seated upon his ass, threw in their faces this sublime defiance, and revealed his divinity, "If these hold their peace, the very stones shall cry out."

The city and the temple were already taking shape in the morning sun. Christ did not turn his eyes from them. His first tears had been for Lazarus. Now it was over the city that he wept. He did not curse it; he unfolded its frightful history; he groaned aloud, "If upon this day thou too hadst known the things that are for thy peace! But now they are hidden from thine eyes. For the days shall come upon thee when thine enemies shall raise up a rampart against thee, and they shall compass thee round and hem thee in on every side; and they shall dash thee to the ground, and thy children within thee, and they shall not leave in thee a stone upon a stone, because thou hast not known the time of thy visitation."

MONDAY OF HOLY WEEK

As that feast approached, Jerusalem teemed with Jews and even with gentiles. "Who is it?" they asked. "We have seen with our eyes. . . . He raised Lazarus at Bethany."

The high priests took counsel. How could Jesus be arrested in the full light of day, in the midst of a fanatical people? Did Judas Iscariot know where his Master spent his nights? For the moment, having just dismounted from the ass, he no longer hid himself. "Sir," several gentiles asked Philip, "we would see Jesus."

UNLESS THE GRAIN DIE . . .

At the moment he was to be found in the temple enclosure, and was proclaiming the hour when the Son of Man would be glorified. But what sombre glory! According to him one must die in order to triumph; to save one's life, one must lose it. "Unless the grain of wheat fall into the ground and die, itself remaineth alone; but if it die, it bringeth forth much fruit. . . ." (The earth already knew the secret of creative renunciation, of suffering that redeems. This mystery is written in nature.)

Immediately after these words, Jesus stopped. We can see his trembling hand move from his forehead to his eyes, as though to shut out the sight, but a few steps away, of that door opening into the darkness beyond. "Now my soul is troubled; and what shall I say?" The man in him was struggling against himself; the lamb smelled the slaughterhouse, did not wish to go forward, resisted. "Father, save me from this hour!" But immediately he caught himself; it was for this agony and this death that he had come. He was no longer speaking to the people, but to himself, to comfort himself, when he burst forth with the victorious cry, "And I, if I be lifted up from the earth, will draw all men to myself." All, even those who would torture him, all things also, even the purified body of Lazarus.

They harassed him with foolish questions. He was going to die, the game was up, and still no one had understood. Here the last days had come; never again would the Author of life touch the earth with his feet, or children's foreheads with his hands. And even yet they were not firm in their belief! At the end of his strength, the vanquished one could only repeat with weakened voice, "I am light! . . . Yet a little while the light is among you. . . . Become sons of light."

TUESDAY AND WEDNESDAY

That evening, as he had promised, he hid himself in Bethany, and the following days he did the same. Perhaps he no longer stayed in the house of Lazarus, long since discovered. Indeed the eastern side of the Mount of Olives, where St. Mark tells us that he took refuge, adjoins Bethany.

On Tuesday morning he again took the road to Jerusalem, and in passing a fig-tree that bore no fruit he cursed it, no doubt to pre-figure the fate of the city.

Every day, nevertheless, he went up again to the Temple (at the cost of what fatigue, before the supreme prostration!). And he began to fight, apparently supported by all the people. To the Pharisees who questioned him as if he were a malefactor, he dared to reply as their judge. Against the tricks of these foxes, he some-times used his divine strategy. If they asked him, "By what authority dost thou these things?" he opposed them with a ques-tion, "The baptism of John—whence was it? Of heaven or of men?" The foxes avoided the question and stammered, "We know not"; for if they had answered, "Of men," they would have stirred up the people who venerated their last prophet. And if they had replied, "Of heaven," he would have answered, "Why then did ye not believe in him?" They therefore stammered that they did not know. Triumphantly Jesus said:

"Neither do I tell you by what authority I do these things."

But the people understood. The furious Pharisees withdrew. Content with his victory, the Rabbi again became familiar as in the early days and told stories, of which now every one of them was beginning to understand the meaning. For example, that concern-ing the man who had two sons and who commanded one to work in the vineyard. At first the son refused, then repented and went out. The other son replied, "I go, sir," and he went not. . . . The humblest of his listeners knew that the father was the heavenly Father and that the prostitutes, the publicans who have repented, are the children of light, but that the Pharisees who had submitted to the Law and yet who betrayed it in their hearts, were accursed.

THE MURDEROUS HUSBANDMEN

Now these same Pharisees were returning. The Lord's tone changed immediately, became aggressive. For it was for them alone, not for the disciples, that three days before his Passion he invented the parable of the murderous husbandmen —so bold, so clear that the high priests wished to seize him at that very hour and would have done so if they had not feared the people.

The man who had let his vineyard sent his servants to the husbandmen to receive his part of the wine, but they fell upon them and beat them, sending them away. "So the Lord of the vineyard said, 'What am I to do? I will send my beloved son; him, maybe, they will reverence.' But the husbandmen upon seeing him reasoned among themselves, saying, 'This is the heir; let us kill him, that the inheritance may become ours.' And casting him out of the vineyard they killed him."

A prophecy so soon to come to pass should have touched their hearts; it was the beloved Son who at that very moment was speaking to the murderous husbandmen; the cross already existed somewhere, in some store-room where gibbets were kept in reserve. Judas fixed the price at thirty pieces of silver; Pilate read the report concerning the tumult caused among the people by a healer from Nazareth. And nevertheless this spavined adventurer, upon whom the synagogue had its eye and who would not go much further now, challenged the crafty specialists in the Scripture, and forced them to read the text. Looking at them Jesus said, "What then meaneth this scripture; 'The stone which the builders rejected, the same is become the corner-stone? Everyone that falleth upon that stone shall be broken to pieces: and upon whomsoever it fall, it shall crush him.' "

If there was in the world at this moment an unforeseen event, literally inconceivable, it was the universal upheaval caused by the skirmishes of a Nazarene preacher with the priests of Jerusalem. The latter were therefore not frightened. But they were aware that they could do nothing without the Romans. The crime of blasphemy did not exist in the eyes of the Romans; they must therefore cause Jesus to fall under suspicion for other reasons. And this was the meaning of that insidious question asked by those sent to ensnare him:

"Is it lawful to give tribute to Cæsar or not?"

RENDER TO CÆSAR . . .

Twenty years earlier, at the moment when they had been annexed to the Empire, another Galilean named Judas had answered the question in the negative, and he had been murdered with his followers. If Jesus had recourse to the famous words, "Render to Cæsar the things that are Cæsar's, and to God the things that are God's," it was because in the drama of Calvary, prearranged from all eternity, it was not fitting that the Romans play any other part than that of executioner, Israel made use of Rome to sacrifice its victim, but the victim first belonged to Israel. Rome, itself, in the person of Pilate, found no fault with Jesus.

But where do the rights of Cæsar end, and where begin the rights of God? This is the source of endless debate. Up to the day when these words were pronounced by a poor rebellious Jew already marked for death, Cæsar was divine and the gods belonged to the Empire far more than the Empire to the gods. Suddenly, above all tyranny, there was raised the power of him who is recognised by free man as the only Lord on earth and in heaven. Thenceforth, although the human conscience would still be subjected to the worst violence, it would none the less be free; martyrdom touches the body, but throughout the centuries all the power of the State would end on the threshold of a sanctified soul.

XXIV

THE WIDOW'S MITE

THE DUEL between the synagogue and the Son of Man was at a standstill. The Pharisees no longer questioned him, fearing to be humiliated before the crowd. Aware of what was being plotted, they bided their time. Sometimes the Nazarene provoked them, saying, "How say they that the Christ is Son of David? David . . . calleth him 'Lord': and how is he his son?" But they avoided answering; they were preparing an answer to be written in blood.

As he awaited his hour, the Son of Man did almost nothing. He spent the time watching the people pass by; scribes, clothed in their long robes, saluted on all sides because of their endless prayers; the faithful who cast their offerings into the treasury. Leaning against a column, in the temple enclosure, Jesus grew angry, and mocked the Pharisees: but he was touched at the sight of the widow who made an offering even though she had little. Of what value were alms which were not made at a sacrifice? Perhaps we have never really given anything?

PROPHECY OF THE RUIN OF THE TEMPLE
AND THE END OF THE WORLD

Thus, during those last hours, Jesus watched the people go by, just as to-day an agitator sought by the police would seat himself at a side-walk café, knowing that he could be arrested at any moment. His attention focused on no particular face, his eyes remained fixed upon the temple. A familiar voice was raised near him, "Master, look, what fine stones! How they are adorned! What buildings!" Then Jesus said:

"For these things which ye behold, the days shall come wherein there shall not be left a stone upon a stone here, that shall not be cast down."

None dared to reply, as they followed him across the Cedron, flowing below the temple, and climbed the Mount of Olives. But there was none among them but was overwhelmed by this prophecy—the worst that could fall upon the ears of a Jew. Finally, all together, they decided to ask him, "Master, when therefore shall these things be and what shall be the sign that they are about to befall?"

The Man-God at the end of his course, already half delivered from time, in which he had been submerged for thirty years, was to speak, without taking time into account; for he was that Jesus, that Lord for whom according to the words of an epistle of Kephas, "one day is as a thousand years, and a thousand years as one day."

Many souls have been troubled by this prophecy of the ruin of the temple and of the city, confused with the end of the world. The faith of many has been shaken by the words, "This generation shall not pass away until all things be accomplished."

The persecution of the Christians, the seige and the ruin of Jerusalem, yes, this generation was to be its witness and its victim. Only the Christians knew how to escape the Roman soldiers and find safety in the mountains, for they had been advised by the Lord, "When ye see Jerusalem being encompassed by armies, then know ye that her desolation is at hand. Then let those in Judæa flee to the mountains. . . . Let not him that is upon the house-top come down to fetch his cloak. . . ."

But between this ruin and the signs in the stars and the roaring of the sea and of the tidal waves which would proclaim the end of the world, Jesus placed only an indeterminate interval: "Jerusalem shall be trampled on by the gentiles, until the season of the gentiles be fulfilled." As he followed with his eternal eye the unfolding of history, Jesus was no longer a man who foresaw the future, but the Son of God who, defying the limits of time, cried out to the Pharisees, "Before Abraham came to be, I am."

And he who knew all things, knew also that his vision was not the same as that of his followers and that it was leading them into error. But this happy error would arm them with hope strong enough to conquer the earth. In their eyes would count as nothing the glories of a world which was doomed and doomed at short shrift. Had they thought that nineteen centuries later Christians would still be awaiting the manifestation of the Son of Man, they might have slept.

To speak truly, by dimming their perspective, the Lord did not deceive them. For each of us the world comes to an end on the day of our death. And it is true, with a particular truth, that none of us knows the day nor the hour when the sun will go out for him, when the moon will cease to bathe the hedgerows of his childhood, when all at once the stars will sink into the immense darkness that will close about him. And it is in the life of each of us that the anti-Christ rises up at the hour we expect him the least, when false prophets come with their poisons, and magicians with their philtres. "Watch ye, for ye know not the day nor the hour." Those virgins are foolish who take no oil with them and who become drowsy because the bridegroom tarries, until they are awakened in the middle of the night by the terrible cry, "Behold, the bridegroom cometh." Terror of sudden death. . . .

And doubtless one day Jesus will shine forth in the clouds in all his power and glory. And on that day, the "season of the gentiles" will be fore-shortened for us as it was in the eyes of Christ, in the days when he was in the flesh. In this light, which will illumine clearly, not so much the destiny of races and kingdoms as that of each human soul in particular, the history of the world will be revealed in countless individual histories. And all the goats will be on the left, and the sheep on the right.

"Then shall the King say to those on his right, 'Come, ye blessed of my Father, inherit the kingdom prepared for you from the foundation of the world. For I was hungry and ye gave me to eat, thirsty and ye gave to drink: I was a stranger and ye brought me within, naked and ye clothed me: I was sick and ye visited me, in prison and ye came unto me.' Then shall the just answer him, saying, 'Lord, when did we see thee hungry and did feed thee, or thirsty and did give thee to drink? When did we see thee a stranger and did bring thee within, or naked and did clothe thee? When did we see thee sick or in prison and did come unto thee?' And the King answering shall say to them, 'Amen, I say to you, inasmuch as ye did it to one of the least of these my brethren, ye did it to me.' "

What glorious hope! There are all those who will discover that their neighbour is Jesus himself, although they belong to the mass of those who do not know Christ or who have forgotten him. And, nevertheless, they will find themselves well loved. It is impossible for any one of those who has charity in his heart not to serve Christ. Even those who think they hate him have consecrated their lives to him, for Jesus is disguised and masked in the midst of men, hidden among the poor, among the sick, among prisoners, among strangers. Many who serve him officially have never known who he was; and many who do not even know his name will hear on the last day the words that open to them the gates of joy: "Those children were I, and I those working-men; I wept on the hospital bed; I was that murderer in his cell, whom you consoled."

XXV

EACH evening brought him back to Bethany. The agony of what he was to suffer, he already tasted. All the Passion passed through his mind; he lived it, blow by blow of the whip, drop by drop of the spittle. He already felt the weight of the cross. Did he see his mother during these last days? Perhaps she emerged at last from her obscurity because he no longer had the strength to repel her. The disciples watched their Master and held their tongues, relying on his promise that no matter what happened, he would return to them, like a man gone away on a voyage, and who, returning, knocks on the door some night or at dawn. . . . Yes, they would wait for him. One evening, one of them was to ask of the others, "Where is Judas?"

Someone answered that their bursar dared not come again to the house in Bethany after what he had said about the perfumed ointment. And Jesus, who doubtless walked last, bent under the weight of the invisible tree, saw in spirit the most reasonable of his disciples at that very moment treating with the conqueror, on a basis of thirty pieces of silver. "For the appearance of the thing," he told them, "not to inconvenience you. . . ."

The last night before that of the agony, Thursday near dawn, Jesus told Peter and John to go to the city to prepare the feast of the Passover. That year the Passover fell upon the sabbath. Why did not Jesus wish to observe the feast on the eve of the Passover, like all other Jews, but rather on the day before? It was simply because he knew that next day he would be the lamb of the sacrifice.

Doubtless a friend had been warned, the friend who waited for the two disciples at the gate of the city. It was understood that he would carry a pitcher of water so that Peter and John would recognise him. In the upper room of his house this one of the brethren had arranged a rug and cushions around the low table, and had ready the ritual lamb which had been sacrificed in the temple.

Jesus walked, absorbed in his love. "Now before the feast of the Passover," writes St. John, "Jesus, knowing that his hour was come that he should pass out of this world to the Father, having loved his own that were in the world, he loved them until the end." Scarcely had they arrived when the Apostles began to dispute their places about him, not knowing what day this was, nor what hour. John sat at his right. The Man of Kerioth must have been the nearest on the other side, since Jesus was able to give him a morsel dipped in the dish.

"With desire have I desired to eat this passover with you before I suffer."

This shoulder upon which a gibbet was to lie, now received the living weight of a head. According to the rite, Jesus blessed the first cup of wine. But the dispute started again. As each laid claim to be the greatest, he reminded them that among them the greatest was to become the least.

"But I am in the midst of you as he that serveth."

And seeking to abase himself still further, he washed their feet, he the Author of life. He washed the feet of Judas who did not protest. Only Peter drew back. Christ had to threaten him, "If I wash thee not, thou hast no part with me." And Peter answered, "Lord, not my feet only, but also my hands and my head."

THE STENCH OF A SOUL

At any other time, Jesus would have smiled. Kephas' pure and simple soul shone forth, but at the same time near him rose an odour of corruption and spiritual death which the Lord could not bear. He could contain himself no longer and murmured:

"Ye are clean, but not all." And he added, "Ye call me Master and Lord; and ye say well, for so I am. If, therefore, I, the Lord and Master, have washed your feet, ye also ought to wash one another's feet."

The stench of this soul tormented him. He could no longer bear its smell. The eleven others had guessed nothing, understood nothing. Perhaps they did not greatly love their pinch-penny comrade. But, after all, he was right to defend the common purse; a little surly, but each man to his own nature. Jesus no longer had the strength to dissimulate:

"Amen, amen, I say to you, one of you will betray me."

These words burst forth in the darkened room where those thirteen Jews reclined, each before his steaming plate. A silence, and each of these poor men questioned himself, examined his conscience and queried the Master, "Is it I? No, it is not I." To the left of Christ, close to his ear, the voice of Judas trembled, "Is it I, Rabbi?"

Not bravado; doubtless he did not yet know, he was still hesitating. In the depths of his being a struggle went on, a despairing struggle in the strongest sense, familiar to many Christians, when the soul, wounded unto death, wrestles with itself, knowing that in the end it will be vanquished. Judas had loved Jesus and perhaps loved him still despite his failure, his venom, his desire not to be linked with the losing side. The thirty pieces of silver were chiefly of value as a symbol of his alliance with the government. At all events, poor Jesus was lost. Judas felt himself slipping; his anguish was not assumed when he asked, "Master, is it I?" Only he could hear the answer spoken in a low voice and which fixed his purpose for ever, "Thou hast said it."

And again the Master gave up his secret, in heart-breaking accents, because he was about to lose one of his little ones, because this Judas was one of those whom he had chosen. Perhaps a little less loved than the others . . . but during those three years there must have been between them occasions when some words of affection were exchanged, some pardon asked and given.

"The Son of Man goeth, as it is written of him; but woe to that man through whom the Son of Man is betrayed! it were good for that man if he had not been born."

In the heavy silence that followed, Peter, who was in the lowest place, beckoned to John, who was reclining upon Jesus' shoulder, and spoke to him. "Say who it is of whom he speaketh." John had but to raise his eyes and but to move his lips to be understood. "Lord, who is it?"

Perhaps Jesus held back from confiding this to anyone else. But he had reached the limits of his life, and in this last halt, what had he still to hide from him whose breathing he felt for the last time (how light his head and how heavy the cross would be!). And so he whispered to him:

"He it is, for whom I shall dip this morsel and give it to him."

And having dipped the bread in the dish, he held out the morsel to Judas, who, seated on his other side, must have heard him. At least he must have seen the head of Christ bent over the head of his chosen disciple. At this very instant "did Satan enter into him." Judas raged with jealousy, too astute not to understand that he was kept at a distance, that as John was the most loved, he had always been the least loved. . . . The Son of Man, before whom stretched all the suffering of the Passion, could not bear the hatred which was suddenly unchained in this unhappy man—the hatred of a fallen angel. This real and substantial presence of Satan in a soul created for love was too great for his remaining strength. He begged him:

"That which thou dost, do quickly."

The others believed that he was sending him to distribute alms or to buy what was needed for the feast. Judas, mad with hatred, arose. Since the Master was sending him to his destiny, why should he resist, he who perhaps had never rested his head upon any shoulder? The heart of Christ had never beaten against his ear. He had been loved just enough for his treason to be inexcusable. His rancour choked him. He opened the door and went out into the night.

THE EUCHARIST

Even those of the Apostles who knew nothing of all this could feel the atmosphere lighten. Perhaps Judas left the door half opened. The Master had lowered his eyes and everyone watched the familiar face that none of them really knew, that was never the same, that was constantly changed by emotions beyond human ken. He held a bit of bread between his fingers. He broke it with his holy and venerable hand, and gave the morsels to them, saying, "Take ye, this is my body."

"And he took a cup, and giving thanks gave to them, and all drank thereof. And he said to them:

" 'This is my blood, of the covenant, which is being shed on behalf of many. Amen, I say to you, that thenceforth I shall not drink of the fruit of the vine until that day when I drink it new in the kingdom of God.' "

What did they understand of this, they who had partaken of this body and this blood? The Son of Man was there, seated at the centre of the table, and at the same time each of them felt him tremble within him, a trembling, the burning of a flame that was but refreshment and delight. For the first time in this world the marvel was consummated; it was given them to possess the loved one, to absorb him in themselves, to nourish themselves with him, to make with him but one substance, to be transformed in his living love.

We can measure the love with which he overwhelmed the disciples in the light of the words that Jesus was now to pronounce, for he called them, "My little children"—these rough men in the prime of life. Tenderness gushed like an issue of blood from his heart that was soon to be opened by a lance:

"Little children, a little while only I am with you; ye shall seek me, and as I said to the Jews, 'Whither I go ye cannot come,' so now I say to you, 'A new commandment I give to you, that ye love one another; that as I have loved you, so ye also love one another. Hereby shall all know that ye are my disciples, if ye have love one for another.' "

And then he spoke to Simon. This very night the Prince of this World would be loosened, and they, the little children, would be sifted like wheat. It would be for him, Peter, once the trial was finished, to strengthen his brethren. Impetuously the Apostle interrupted that he was ready to go with Jesus, even to prison, even to death. In him, Jesus foresaw at this moment the bitterest drop of the chalice that he was to drink. For this man, the strongest of them all, who cried out in a transport of confidence and love, at the dawn of the next day would deny him thrice. Jesus warned him softly. But Peter, beside himself, insisted:

"Though I should have to die with thee, I will not deny thee."

All the others protested with Kephas. They had left the table and surrounded Jesus, whose gaze, above their heads, focused upon that naked tree uplifted in the midst of the world's darkness, the goal he was to touch at last. The eleven now understood that the good days were at an end, and there were to be no more miracles to astound the Jews. Without effort they put on a brave front. "Behold, Lord, there are two swords here. . . ." Jesus shrugged his shoulders: "Enough!" It was not swords, but faith, that they needed. "Let not your heart be troubled." They knew where he was going, and they knew the way. . . . Thomas' wondering voice was raised:

"Lord, we know not whither thou goest; how can we know the way?"

Up to the very end they took every word in its most material sense. Jesus said to him:

"I am the way and the truth and the life; no one goeth to the Father save through me."

And as Philip interrupted him, "Lord, show us the Father, and it is enough for us," Jesus answered him:

"So long a time have I been with you, and thou dost not know me, Philip? He that hath seen me, hath seen my Father."

He was no longer irritated by this lack of intelligence which he could not conquer but which the Spirit was to overcome. The little group gathered closer around him. Like all men afraid of death, they behaved like children fearful of the night. And the Son of Man whose love had burst forth at other times in violent and bitter words, already broken, already bent before the first blow, before the first stroke of the scourge, took them under his wing and warmed them with tender and portentous words in which the Man and God was revealed again and again. And he introduced them into the mystery of Union.

"I will not leave you orphans; I am coming to you. Yet a little while, and the world beholdeth me no more; but ye behold me, because I live and ye shall live. In that day ye shall know that I am in the Father, and ye in me, and I in you. He that hath my commandments and keepeth them, he it is that loveth me; and he that loveth me shall be loved by my Father, and I will love him and manifest myself to him. . . . If any one loveth me, he will keep my word, and my Father shall love him, and we will come to him and make our abode with him."

A great calm now descended upon them, and they were no longer afraid. They were the friends of Jesus, united to him and in him. Already they tasted the overflowing heritage that he had promised them: his burning peace.

"Peace I leave to you, my peace I give to you; not as the world giveth do I give to you. Let not your heart be troubled, neither let it be dismayed."

The hour was drawing near. He could not longer remain in the place. "Arise, let us go." He led them from the room, stopping for a moment in the entrance way. Never before had he spoken to them as on this night. Now they knew that their friend was God and that God was Love. And he who had rested his head upon the shoulder of the Son of Man preserved each word for all time.

"I am the vine, ye the branches. . . . As my Father hath loved me, I also have loved you; abide in my love . . . that my joy may be in you."

What need did they have of understanding anything more? All of the New Law was contained in one word, the most profaned word in all the languages of the world—Love.

L

"This is my commandment, that ye love one another as I have loved you. Greater love than this no one hath, than that he lay down his life for his friends."

They had not chosen him, their adored Master; it was he who had chosen them from all the world. The world that had been rejected would hate them, as it hated Christ. They were to be persecuted for their love, but the Spirit would be upon them.

The eleven were again troubled because he had said, "A little while and ye behold me no more; and again a little while, and ye shall see me." Full of pity, Jesus sought to assure them in advance of the joy that would be theirs in drinking and eating with him after he had risen:

"Amen, amen, I say to you, that yourselves shall weep and lament, but the world shall rejoice; ye shall be sorrowful, but your sorrow shall be turned into joy. A woman when she is in travail hath sorrow, because her hour hath come; but when she hath brought forth her child, she remembereth no more her anguish, for the joy that a man hath been born into the world."

They were inflamed by these words. It was with a sort of drunkenness that they interrupted him, "Behold, now thou speakest plainly, and utterest no parable. Now we know that thou knowest all things, and that thou needest not that any one question thee; for this reason we believe that thou camest forth from God."

The Son of Man, who for three years had suffered from their lack of faith, their slowness of understanding, took little joy in this outburst. He sighed, "Do ye now believe?" And suddenly, in a hard voice:

"Behold, the hour cometh, and is now come, that ye shall be scattered, every man to his own, and myself ye shall leave alone."

But before these poor, saddened faces, he drew up short. No, he was not angry at his loved ones. All the misery that was to overwhelm them he knew and suffered already. The eleven were to be the weakest on this night when the stricken Master would touch them on the shoulder. And yet how suddenly he drew himself up, this Nazarene from the lower classes, whom the soldiers were seeking, this outlawed Jew who was to be covered with their spit! In what sovereign tones he issued the challenge which beyond his judges, beyond his executioners, even beyond Tiberius Cæsar, was like the trumpeting of an angel on this night:

"Nevertheless, have courage, I have overcome the world!"

SACERDOTAL PRAYER

He had overcome the world, but he had drawn apart from the world the little troop of those who would not perish. And for this he gave glory to the Father, at the entrance to the arena, on the threshold of night (the first of those countless brethren who, because of hatred of his Name, would be delivered to the Beast). Before going forward, he communed with himself and prayed.

An infinite mystery is clothed in this little phrase repeated several times in the Gospels, "Jesus withdrew a little way to pray. . . ." He prayed to the Father, he who was consubstantia with the Father. Can we understand this? We are created in the image of God, and all meditation brings us back to the centre of our own being, as though it were we who speak to ourselves. So the humblest Christian, after Communion, or simply in the state of grace, and who praises the presence of the three Persons, cannot withdraw into himself without being identified with the God within him.

There is an analogy which helps us thus to meditate upon this mystery—the prayer of the Man-God who was but one with him to whom he prayed.

He spoke to himself and at the same time to another. But this time, on the edge of darkness, a creature assisted at the dialogue of the Father and the Son; a young man, John the son of Zebedee. Perhaps he was not able to hear the words distinctly. Perhaps it was given him to take part in this silent meditation and, without the silence being broken, the prayer of the adored Master was engraved, verse after verse, in the heart of the listening disciple.

He alone remembered it, doubtless because he was alone to hear this prayer. Not that he was better than the others; he was the most violent, the most devoted. Only the day before, this "Son of Thunder" had demanded a throne for himself and his brother, sought to benefit because he felt himself preferred. Moreover, there were other childish audacities of the kind that people overlook. One day he interrupted his Master to express pride at having forbidden a man to drive out demons in the name of Jesus, as though Jesus belonged to him alone! He was a young man, and this means he was greedy, violent, cruel, even to the point of willing a fire from heaven to exterminate that town of Samaria which had not wished to receive him.

Nevertheless, he was preferred; he was the young man whom Jesus loved, but who was not rich like the other young man whom Jesus loved, and who did not have great possessions (although he came of the best family of all the disciples, his father Zebedee having men in his employ, and John seems to have been an intimate in the house of the high priest). His was the most supple mind, the most open; we may go further and say that the disciple whom Jesus loved was full of genius. Like most of the saints from Paul to the early fathers of the Church, like Augustine, like Bonaventure, like Thomas, like Francis, like John of the Cross, but even more than these, he was filled with the gifts of the Spirit.

Was this intelligence, sharpened by love, enough to introduce him into the mystery of the last prayer of the Son of God? Perhaps not, but his head had just lain on the Lord's bosom; and for that infinite moment he had become another. The Son of Thunder would thenceforth be the son of Love, he who during the Last Supper had rested his forehead on the heart of God, had surprised a secret which he would never forget: what his eyes had seen, what his hands had touched, what his ears had heard, concerning the Word of Life.

The triumphant words which John has handed down to

us are surprising as they come so soon before the prostration and the anguish of Gethsemani. The prayer of Christ which John recalled shone with tranquil certainty, as if the Lord took advantage of this last minute before all his power would be swallowed up in darkness: "Father, the hour is come: glorify thy Son, in order that the Son may glorify thee: even as thou hast given him power over all flesh. . . . Now this is everlasting life, that they know thee, the only true God, and him whom thou hast sent, Jesus Christ. . . . For them I pray; not for the world do I pray, but for them thou hast given me, because they are thine."

For a moment he gazed upon this ocean of sorrow on whose shores he now stood; then his eyes turned to contemplate his eternal handiwork: that indefectible union of sanctified creatures and of their God in the person of the Son, "that they may be one as we are one—I in them, and thou in me—that they may be perfected in unity."

But what are the frontiers of this world for which he does not pray? And what will be the eternal destiny of that rejected world?

XXVI

GETHSEMANI

THE TIME HAD COME to go out into the night. When he had crossed this threshold, his Passion would begin. He recited the *hallel* which is the Pascal thanksgiving and pushed open the door. He went down, skirting around the temple walls, lighted by the Pascal moon, and reached an enclosed plot of land at the foot of the Mount of Olives. Since Jesus had been a fugitive the little troop often slept in this garden, called Gethsemani because of an oil press which was to be found there. It was their habitual refuge when they could not push on to Bethany.

On that night the eleven did nothing that seemed extraordinary to them. According to their custom, they slept upon the earth wrapped in their cloaks. The Master took with him Peter, James and John and went apart to pray, but this was as usual, and did not surprise them.

At a stone's throw from his three dearest friends, Jesus fell, his face upon the ground. He was afraid; yes, he must also know fear. The smell of blood made him shudder; he felt his body shrink from the physical torture that lay before him. "Father, if thou wilt, turn aside this cup from me!"

One part of his being shrank from his terrible destiny. "Yet not my will but thine be done. . . ." For at this moment his own will was to escape from the horror before him.

He withdrew a damp hand from his forehead. Whence came this blood? The supplication stopped on his lips; he listened. At certain hours of life, in the silence of the night, every man has experienced the indifference of matter which is blind and deaf. This matter crushed Christ. In his flesh he felt the horror of an infinite absence. The Creator had withdrawn and creation was but the bottom of an empty sea; the dead stars were scattered in space; in the darkness he could hear the cries of beasts being devoured.

Then this Jew, blotted against the earth, crushed to the ground, arose. The Son of God was abased so low that he had need of human consolation. His turn had come, he thought, to rest his bloody head upon a friendly bosom. He therefore rose and approached the three sleeping men ("sleeping for sorrow," says St. Luke).

But they were overcome by sleep. Sleep had won over all their love—and this is something we also know. Jesus, prisoner of his humanity, at that moment when he had greatest need of his friends' support, was thrown by them against that law of torpor and sleep. Even the beloved Apostle slept with all the strength of his youth; one might say his own strength had overcome him.

"Could ye not then watch one hour with me?"

They arose, sighed a little, fell back. The Master dragged himself to the place he had already marked with his blood, knelt once more, held out his hands like a blind man, until again he was thrown back upon his friends—for, insensible as they were, they were there, he could shake them, touch their hair. Thus, the Son of Man became a pendulum swinging between man's torpor and God's absence; from the absent Father to the sleeping friends.

The third time that he dragged himself toward them, he saw that they were arising, their eyes still closed, not knowing what to say. If the moon still shone, perhaps Christ saw their poor faces, swollen and disfigured, covered with beard.

"Sleep on now, and rest!"

Now he needed no one but himself. He remained motionless, his face no longer against the earth, nor bent over sleeping men. He heard their sighs, their snoring, and beyond, the confused sound of steps, of voices. . . . And finally:

"Arise, let us go; behold, he that betrayeth me is at hand."

Hastening, they rejoined the other disciples and awakened them. Then all pressed about him, and he was lost in their midst. The tribune which came out this night with the attendants of the high priest and some soldiers of the cohort, carrying torches, saw in the light of the flames naught but a quiet little group of Jews, and among them there was none who seemed to stand out or to dominate. The Author of life was one of those bearded Nazarenes, undistinguishable from the others since it was necessary for Judas to point him out. The Man of Kerioth had the idea of kissing him, "Whomsoever I shall kiss, that is he."

This idea of the traitor must have come from some supernatural and devilish source. This betrayal by a kiss bewildered even him who expected all. This mouth on his cheek! He said, "Friend, for what a purpose art thou come!" And as the soldiers surrounded him, "Thou betrayest the Son of Man with a kiss?" Until the end this creature astonished him. He thought he had touched the depths of human baseness; but this kiss . . .

At first there was a tumult. At first the Apostles did not show cowardice, because they knew their Master was all-powerful; and as Kephas with his sword cut off the ear of Malchus, the servant of the high priest, Jesus ordered him to put up his sword into the scabbard. He brushed the Apostles aside and, like a mother, came forward, swelling himself up to cover his brood: "It is I! let them go! When I was daily with you in the temple ye stretched not forth your hands against me. But this is your hour."

In the light of the torches, the pack threw themselves upon the willing prey. Then all left him and fled save a strange young man who had come there without even taking time to clothe himself. We do not know the name of him who showed this last mark of fidelity! They seized him: but like the agile boy he was, he left behind his wrap and escaped from them.

Jesus was brought to Annas (father-in-law of Caiaphas, the high priest) who had him bound more tightly and sent him to his son-in-law. Caiaphas was waiting with the elders of the people and several members of the Sanhedrin. Perhaps they had never seen Jesus. The miracle-worker, the enemy of the high priests, was this he, this poor wretch? All the same, Caiaphas questioned him at first with that tone of prudent benignity which, many centuries later, was adopted by the judges of Jeanne d'Arc. The accused man replied that he had spoken openly before the world, in the synagogue and in the temple, and that he had spoken nothing in secret.

"Why dost thou question me? Question those who have heard what I said to them; behold, they know what things I said."

Had he raised his voice a little? Despite himself, did he still speak as master? The first blow fell upon his face, from the thick hand of a soldier.

"Answerest thou thus the high priest?"

"If I have spoken ill, bear witness against the evil; but if well, why strikest thou me?"

Some foundation must be shown for the accusations against him. Two men bore witness that the accused had claimed to be able to destroy the temple of God and to rebuild it in three days. The high priest arose, "Answerest thou naught?"

KEPHAS' DENIAL

As the night declined, it grew cold. A great fire, lighted by the servants, burned in the courtyard. All those who were roaming about outside the palace, awaiting the dawn, approached the flames. From the gloom emerged a circle of figures and of outstretched hands. A maidservant was struck by a bearded face which she thought she recognised: "This man too was with him." Peter started: "Woman, I know him not."

He had entered into the courtyard, thanks to a disciple who knew the portress of the high priest. Suspicious, the woman had said to him, "Art thou also one of his disciples?" and already Peter had denied it. Now he drew away from the fire so as not to be recognised. A first hoarse cock announced the dawn; but trembling with cold and fear, he did not hear it. Again they gathered about him: "Truly thou also art one of them, for thy very speech doth manifest thee."

More dangerous was the witness brought by a kinsman of

Malchus, "Did I not see thee in the garden?" Peter, terrified, protested, swore with oaths that he did not know the man; and such were his imprecations that his accusers hesitated and went back to warm themselves, leaving him alone. The heavens grew pale. Again a cock crowed. Dawn came also to this poor heart. The night was over, all became clear within him, as the roofs of the palace and houses, the tops of the olive trees and the highest palms gradually emerged from the darkness. Then a door was opened. Pushed ahead by the attendants, a man appeared, his wrists tied together, a jail- and gallows-bird. He looked at Peter. In his gaze there was held an infinite treasure of tenderness and pardon. With horror the Apostle looked upon this face already swollen by blows from fists. He hid his own face between his hands, and going out, wept more tears than he had ever shed since he had come into the world.

Jesus had come to the time when he would be spat upon. This had begun when Caiaphas had called on him to answer, "I adjure thee by the living God to tell us whether thou art the Christ . . . the Son of the Blessed One." Then the silent man had held himself erect and said distinctly:

"I am; and ye shall see the Son of Man seated on the right of the Power and coming with the clouds of heaven."

There was a cry of horror. And some began to spit on him, and then others. Then the attendants struck him. They covered his face and hit him with their fists. "Prophesy to us, O Christ, who was it that struck thee?"

If he had not been humble in aspect, if there had been in his bearing that majesty which we attribute to him, the rabble would have held their distance. No, there was nothing in the Nazarene to impress this cowardly scum from the kitchens.

. . . At least not at that moment. Even an ordinary man has so many visages! The silent glory of the Transfiguration must at certain times have shone forth on that august Face which is revealed to us by the photograph of the Holy Shroud of Turin. If our souls are seen in our faces, what must have been that of the Son of God! But doubtless he wished to obscure this Face.

His will to efface himself masked on the Holy Face all that could make the executioners hesitate. It is true that the very purity of a countenance sometimes attracts hate and brings down insults. These brutes had God at their mercy, and they made sport of him to their hearts' content.

The Passion could have ended with Jesus being spat upon. His abjection is already more than our feeble faith can bear. And yet the power of Jesus over souls is rooted in his conformity to the suffering of men; and not only with the normal sorrows of our human condition. There must never be in the world a prisoner, a martyr, a condemned person, innocent or guilty, who does not find in Jesus, outraged and crucified, his own image and likeness. Since he suffered and died, men have not become less cruel, no less blood has been spilled, but the victims have been recreated a second time in the image and likeness of God—even without knowing it, even without willing it.

JUDAS' DESPAIR

While they dragged him away from the attendants to take him to the prætorium (no doubt to the Fortress Antonia which overlooked the Temple) a terrified man surveyed his handiwork. There are no monsters; Judas had not believed that things would go very far—imprisonment, perhaps several stripes from the scourge, and the carpenter would be sent back to his bench. Very little would have been needed for the tears of Judas to be allied in the memory of mankind with those of Peter. He might have become a saint, the patron of all of us who constantly betray Christ. He was stifled with remorse; the gospel says clearly that he "repented." He brought back the thirty pieces of silver to the high priests and confessed, "I have sinned in betraying innocent blood." Judas was on the border of perfect contrition. God might still have had the traitor needed for the Redemption . . . and a saint besides.

What did the thirty pieces of silver mean to Judas? Perhaps he would not have delivered Jesus up if he had not loved him, had not felt himself less loved than the others. The miserable calculations of avarice would not have been sufficient to determine him. At the very moment when the head of John rested on the heart of the Lord, Satan was able to enter into his eternal reign over the heart of Judas.

"And flinging the pieces of silver into the temple, he . . . went away and hanged himself." The Devil has gained nothing over the last of criminals who still hopes. While there exists a ray of hope in the most guilty soul, it is separated from infinite love by only a sigh. And it is the mystery of mysteries that the son of perdition did not heave this sigh.

The priests did not wish to touch this money, which was the price of blood, and used it to buy a potter's field for the burial of strangers. They killed the Son of God and thought only of not contaminating themselves! Thus, on the eve of the Passover, they did not dare to penetrate into the prætorium for fear of soiling their feet, and the Procurator himself was forced to come out and deal with them from the peristyle. Here is an example of the stupidity of the letter, the letter which kills—in the name of which so many lambs have been sacrificed, beginning with the Lamb of God.

PILATE

Pilate hated and distrusted the Sanhedrin, and Herod Antipas as well, but he feared them. In Rome he had been the loser in a dispute with the Jews concerning the golden shields which he had hung in the royal palace in Jerusalem and which he was forced to carry back to Cæsarea, into his own residence. Since he had lost this suit, the Procurator was wary of these furious people: "Take him yourselves, and judge him according to your law."

Now these same Jews who feared to soil themselves in touching the ground of the prætorium where they had gone to have an innocent man condemned to death, professed that it was not lawful for them to put anyone to death. They delivered Jesus up to be crucified, but they would not pronounce the sentence. Pharisaism, so furiously denounced by Christ for three years, now unmasked itself in its most hideous aspect.

Pilate, no doubt exasperated, but prudent, went back into the prætorium. He did not know what question to put to this wretched man, safe for the moment from the clutches of the filthy rabble. It would be too much to say that the Procurator yielded to pity. He knew already it was best to flatter the mania of madmen:

"Art thou the King of the Jews?"

But the Illuminated One answered, "Sayest thou this of thyself, or have others told it thee about me?"

But no, this was not a madman! Pilate fumed—"Am I a Jew?" humiliated at being mixed up in the affair of this fanatic.

Nevertheless the man spoke:

"My kingdom is not of this world. Had my kingdom been of this world, my servants would have fought that I should not be delivered to the Jews. But no, my kingdom is not hence. . . . Thou sayest it, I am a king. For this was I born, and for this am I come into the world, that I may witness to the truth."

Pilate said to him, "What is truth?" If he had had the heart of a beggar, of a lost woman, of a publican, he might have received this reply, "I am the truth, who speaks with thee." But he was a serious man, a great official; he would have shrugged his shoulders. A secret virtue was acting within him, however; this man "had something" . . . he could not say what. He no longer took him for a madman. It was envy that had exasperated the Sanhedrin. One could not deny the power of the prisoner's look, of his voice. This Roman distrusted the Jews, but he was superstitious. One never knew; the Orient was full of dangerous divinites. Indeed his wife had had a dream about this just man, and had told him to have nothing to do with the affair. Why not set him free? Unfortunately, the members of the Sanhedrin had placed themselves on political ground. Jesus declared himself king and Messiah, and it was just this kind of agitator who was most detested in Rome. Pilate's enemies knew it and would turn a powerful arm against him. An insignificant affair, but one which might prove his undoing. He was a politician, and like all politicians who are playing both sides, he sought a subterfuge. Suddenly, he struck his forehead: he had found it. A Nazarene? Well, then Jesus was of Herod's jurisdiction! Since, without Herod's permission, Pilate had massacred some Galilean revolutionaries, he had been at odds with the Tetrarch, but he would show him this mark of deference, and would kill two birds with one stone. He would get rid of Jesus, and would reconcile himself with Herod who happened to be in Jerusalem for the feast.

JESUS BEFORE HEROD

The murderer of John the Baptist had long sought to see this famous Jesus, and received him at first with some pomp, surrounded by his guard and his court. Although the aspect of the unhappy man must have confounded him he proceeded to ply him with questions. But the Son of Man had changed into a statue, and despite the vehement accusations of the scribes, he answered naught to this *fox*, as he had one day called Herod. The Tetrarch and his court about him were the world which Jesus execrated. The priests were less repugnant to him than these futile criminals, these parrots, this scum who believed themselves the flower of the world:

"No! is this Jesus? What a disappointment. He merits death for this if for nothing else."

"But they told me he was handsome! He is frightful! He certainly does not look like a Prophet! What a trumpery affair."

"Strange how reputations are made!"

At least John the Baptist had been somebody. Beside John the Baptist this man did not exist. He was a nobody in comparison. He was an impostor!

"No, but look at his air! Who does he think he is, the poor devil. . . ."

"He thinks he is impressing us with his silence. . . ."

Played out, and unable to get a word out of him, Herod in mockery had him clothed in a white robe and sent him back to Pilate—to his friend Pilate.

BARABBAS

This high official had to find another way out, and believed that he had found it when someone reminded him that it was the custom on the feast of the Passover to release a prisoner selected by the multitude. The Procurator, therefore, came out again and the people ceased their cries in order to hear him:

"I have not found any guilt in this man. . . . But ye have a custom . . . will ye, therefore, that I release unto you the King of the Jews?"

What stupidity to call Jesus thus even in irony! Beside themselves, the scribes and the priests spread their orders everywhere; the people must demand the release of the robber Barabbas. A cry went up, as though from a single throat:

"Barabbas! Barabbas!"

Pilate beat a retreat, seeking to save the innocent Christ from these furious men. As he could hit upon nothing, his Roman indulgence inspired him with a horrible stratagem: to reduce the man to such a state of abjection and misery that no one would any longer attach the slightest importance to his derisory kingdom. It was to save him from the band of wolves that he delivered him over to the soldiers. He knew how the latter would acquit themselves of their task. When he had left their hands the King of the Jews would disarm even the members of the Sanhedrin; he would fill even the bloodthirsty priests with pity.

THE FLAGELLATION

The soldiers, therefore, took hold of him; they were going to amuse themselves. The whips contained balls of lead. All our kisses, all our embraces, the prostitution of the body created to be the dwelling of Love, the debasement of the flesh, crimes not only against grace but against nature, the Son of Man assumed them all himself. The blood with which he was covered, enveloped him with a first scarlet mantle over which the soldiers were to cast another, this one made of cloth, which stuck to the raw flesh. On the ground there were fire kindlings, faggots of a thorny wood. "Wait until I make a crown for the King! Here, put this reed into his hands. . . . Hail to the King of the Jews!" And bending their knees and jostling one another they worshipped him, and fists beat down upon the face that was now but an open wound.

ECCE HOMO

When the Roman saw what remained of the Jew he was reassured. The soldiers had done their work well; this lamentable creature would put to shame those who had delivered him up. He went out to speak to them in person (with an air which said, "You are going to see what you are going to see!"):

"Behold, I bring him forth to you, that ye may know that I find no crime in him."

He went in to find him and reappeared, pushing before him that puppet-like figure covered with red and faded finery, his head crowned with thorns, his face a mask of spittle, of sweat and blood, in which were matted the meshes of his hair.

"Behold the man."

They did not fall to their knees. Where were the lepers he had cured, those he had delivered from devils, the blind whose eyes he had opened? Before this human derelict many of those who had believed in him, still hoping against hope, lost what faith was left to them. Let him be swept out! Take him away! To have believed in this! What shame!

A tremendous cry, "Crucify him," disconcerted the Procurator. He tried to cry out louder than they, "But he is innocent." Then a priest came apart from the multitude. A great silence reigned because he spoke in the name of all.

"We have a law, and according to the law he must die, because he hath made himself Son of God."

Pilate was troubled. *Son of God*—what did this mean? He turned back into the prætorium, made Jesus come forward, and asked him this surprising question, "Whence art thou?"

In the mind of the Procurator there was no question of Jesus' earthly origin. No doubt the Roman sensed in this derelict an immense force which escaped him. But Christ was silent. Pilate grew impatient; did the man not know that his judge had the power to crucify him or to release him?

"Thou wouldst have no power over me, were it not given thee from above; for this cause he that hath delivered me to thee hath the greater sin."

"After this Pilate sought to release him. But the Jews shouted aloud, saying, 'If thou release this man, thou art no friend of Cæsar's: every one who maketh himself a king setteth himself against Cæsar.' When therefore Pilate heard these words, he brought Jesus out, and sat down on the judgment seat, at a place called in Greek *Lithostrotos*, but in Hebrew *Gabbatha*. Now it was the preparation of the passover, about the sixth hour. And he saith to the Jews, 'Behold your King!' They therefore shouted, 'Away with him, away with him, crucify him!' Pilate said to them, 'Am I to crucify your King?" The chief priests answered, 'We have no king but Cæsar.' "

A threatening answer. Pilate understood that he had gone too far, that he could not spare this miserable man without being denounced in Rome. The man found a subterfuge to acquit himself of legal responsibility. This was to wash his hands in public, and to proclaim himself innocent of the blood of this just man. It was for the Jews to reply to this. The rabble cried out, "His blood be upon us and upon our children!" It was, it is still, but the malediction is not eternal: Israel's place is kept at the right hand of the Son of David.

M

THE WAY OF THE CROSS

It was the killing, the stag was delivered over to the dogs. How was he to carry his cross, he who could scarcely drag himself along? Simon of Cyrene, father of the two disciples, Alexander and Rufus, was compelled to help him carry it. Two robbers walking with him, dragging the same wood, could not be distinguished from God. This cross we must see it as it was, so different from the throne which we have built since, and which raises the Lamb of God high above the world! The truth is almost unbearable, we must dare to look it in the face. "The first Christians had a horror of seeing Christ shown upon a cross," writes Père Lagrange, "because with their own eyes they had seen those poor bodies, completely naked, attached to a heavy stake surmounted, in form of a T, by a transverse bar, hands nailed to this gibbet, feet also fixed with nails, the body sinking beneath its own weight, the head hanging, dogs drawn by the odour of blood devouring the feet, buzzards wheeling over this scene of carnage, and the sufferer exhausted by torture, burning with thirst, calling on death with inarticulate cries. It was the punishment of slaves and bandits. It was that which Jesus suffered."

Golgotha was at the very gates of the city. Was there sufficient distance for the three falls of Christ of which tradition tells us? It was but a short way that he advanced, stifled by the crowd, dragged by the soldiers. Perhaps Mary was not within range of his vision, but she was there. She took advantage of the fact that her son and her God had no longer strength nor voice to repel her; at last she emerged from the silence and shadows, with that sword in her heart. No saint could embrace the cross more closely than the Virgin. She espoused the Redemption in silence. No, the Mother did not cry out, for she is not named among the women who wept about the condemned man. As for himself, at this moment he measured beyond his own sufferings the chastisement of his city and of his people, and he trembled for them.

"Weep over yourselves and over your children!" Perhaps one of the weeping women came apart from the others and wiped his face with a veil. Veronica is not known to the evangelists. But she existed; she was not a fictitious personage. It is not possible that a woman could have resisted the desire to wipe that terrible face.

THE CRUCIFIXION

The most awful moment had come: the cloth of the mantle stripped from his wounds, the blows of the hammer upon the nails, the raising of the tree, the weight of the human fruit, thirst quenched with vinegar, with myrrh and with gall, nakedness, the shame of the poor butchered flesh. . . . O refuge of the little Host! The butchers did their butcher's work; they added nothing to it; Jesus prayed for them because they knew not what they did. But nothing put an end to the hate of the scribes and the priests. They were still there, before that living wound, laughing, wagging their heads, mocking; their triumph knew no end. "Others he saved, himself he cannot save. Let the Christ, the King of Israel, come down now from the cross, that we may see and believe."

There was one shadow over their pleasure—the inscription which Pilate had had put upon the gibbet: *This is the King of the Jews.* They attempted to appeal to the Procurator that this be corrected to read, *He said I am the King of the Jews.* But the Procurator's patience had reached the end, he was perhaps torn with anguish. He listened to them drily: what was written, was written.

The multitude milled around this gibbet so close to the earth that the condemned man could still be spat upon. They mocked him saying, "Thou that overthrowest the temple and in three days buildest it up! Save thyself!"

Let him save himself—they but asked to believe in him. Those who loved him huddled together, mounted guard about his exposed body, covering, veiling with their love his nakedness, too bloody, too pitiful, to offend any gaze. Through blood and pus,

he saw his sorrow reflected in beloved faces: that of Mary his
mother, of Mary Magdalene, of one of his aunts, the wife of
Cleophas. Perhaps John's eyes were closed. And here is the
sublime episode, the last invention of innocent and crucified love,
reported by Luke alone: "One of the crucified criminals railed at
him: 'Art thou not the Christ? Save thyself and us!' But the other
in answer rebuked him and said, 'Dost thou not even fear God,
seeing that thou art under the same sentence? And ourselves indeed
justly, for we are receiving the fitting reward of our deeds; but this
man hath done naught amiss.' " Hardly had he spoken when a
great grace was given to him, that of believing that this dying man,
this miserable and rejected man of whom even the dogs wished no
more, was Christ, the Son of God, the Author of life, the King of
Heaven. And he said to Jesus:

"Jesus, remember me when thou comest in thy kingdom."

"This day thou shalt be with me in paradise."

A lone movement of pure love, and a whole life of crime was
blotted out. Good thief, holy labourer of the eleventh hour, fill us
with hope!

DEATH

Out of the depths of his sufferings, Jesus embraced in one
look the two beings he had most loved in this world, and
he confided them to one another: "Woman, behold thy son
—Behold thy Mother"—and ours, for eternity. Mary and John
were never again to leave one another. And then suddenly came
the unexpected cry, which still chills our blood:

"My God, my God, why hast thou forsaken me?"

It was the first verse of the twenty-first Psalm—of that Psalm
which Christ was to fulfil until his death. Yes, we believe with all
our faith that it was necessary for the Son to know that ultimate
horror: abandonment by the Father. But it is not less likely that his
dying thoughts were fixed upon that Psalm whose verses were
accomplished in him to the letter, at that very moment: "But I am
a worm, and no man: the reproach of men, and the outcast of the

people. All they that saw me have laughed me to scorn: they have
spoken with the lips, and wagged the head. He hoped in the Lord,
let him deliver him: let him save him, seeing he delighteth in
him." . . . "They have dug my hands and feet. . . . They parted my
garments amongst them; and upon my vesture they cast lots."

All this was accomplished; lots were cast for the seamless
tunic. The dying Christ had conformed to all that had been
predicted of him. He clung to it with his last strength. But
abandonment he knew at Gethsemani. Many times during those
last three crushing years he must have cried out the words of the
first verse of Psalm xxi, just as we ourselves say "My God!" when
we sigh with fatigue and suffering. The strangest thing is that on
hearing him cry "Eli! Eli!" the soldiers believed that he was calling
upon Elias, and said, "Let be, let us see whether Elias be coming
to save him." These simple people, then, retained a little faith.
Nevertheless the man of sorrows went over his part, verse by verse.
He spoke again, "I thirst!" A sponge dipped in vinegar was held to
his mouth. This was not done out of cruelty; this vinegar was used
by the soldiers and must have been like what is known as *posca* (a
mixture of water and vinegar drunk by soldiers and labourers).
Jesus said: "It is finished."

"And bowing his head, he gave up his spirit." But first he
uttered that great, mysterious cry, which made a centurion strike
his breast, saying; "Truly, he was the Son of God." No words were
necessary; if it pleases the Creator, a cry is sufficient for his
creature to recognise him.

THE ENTOMBMENT

Nothing remained of this dark adventure of three years but the
bodies of the three executed criminals at the entrance to a city,
under a stormy sky, on a dark spring day. An ordinary spectacle,
for it was the custom to leave the bodies of the guilty exposed to
the gaze of all and to the outrage of beasts, at the city gates. But on
the day of the Preparation it was not permissible for these corpses

to remain. Therefore, at the request of the Jews and upon the order of Pilate, the soldiers finished off the two thieves by breaking their legs. As Jesus was already dead, it was enough to pierce his side with a lance which opened his heart: and John, his head leaning perhaps against the broken body, saw water and blood coming from the open wound and felt it flow upon him.

A secret disciple of Jesus, one of those who had been afraid of the Jews when Jesus was living, Joseph of Arimathæa, obtained from the Procurator leave to take away the body. Nicodemus, a politician, who had also been afraid, came forward at that moment with about a hundred pounds of myrrh and aloes. It was the hour of the timid. The two men who had not dared to confess the living Christ and who came to see him secretly in the night, now that he was dead showed more faith and tenderness than those who had expressed themselves in words. Nothing now meant anything to them, these ambitious men, for they had lost Jesus. What did they fear? The Jews could no longer harm them. Everything could be taken from them, now that they had lost everything; those honours to which they cleaved more than anything in the world were as nothing to them now that Jesus was dead.

Joseph of Arimathæa had a new tomb in a garden upon the slope of Golgotha. Because the feast was near at hand, they laid in it the body of the Lord.

XXVII

CLOUDS DULLED THE SKY. Perhaps it is true that the dead came forth, although no one remembered this until later. I imagine rather a spring evening like all evenings in the spring, the smell of warm, damp earth, and that fleshly weariness, that emptiness which I felt as a child, after the death of the last bull, when the arena was emptied, as though my own blood had been impoverished with all the blood that had been shed. An account was settled, the business was finished: and so much hate, henceforth useless, fell back upon the hearts of the scribes. The immense sadness of their race crushed down upon them: enough to fill century after century with dissatisfaction, with a sense of unfulfilment. The Pharisees were still anxious concerning the agitation going on about the body, even one so dishonoured as this had been. Those who had always seen things clearly sneered at those who had been impressed by the impostor. But the Passover was at hand and each went back to his house.

And where were the friends of the vanquished one? What remained of their faith? The Son of Man had entered into death, and by what a gate! To the Jews his memory would be not only abominable but ignoble. His heritage, of which he had said so much, a sign of abjection. His victory over the world? Those who hated him had trapped him, convicted him of lack of power and therefore a fraud before all the people. No—there was nothing for his friends to do but to hide themselves, to conceal their tears, their shame, to keep silence and to wait.

Nevertheless they waited, remembering certain words, leaning upon them; their faith vacillated, but not their love. Perhaps among them some hearts burned, prey to the folly of confidence, which was already the folly of the cross. The women, especially, all those Marys. . . . As for the mother of Jesus there was no need for her to have confidence, she *knew*. But the Passion went on within her. The blows continued to rain down, the spittle to stain the adored face. In her heart she could not stop the shedding of the divine blood. Each cry still vibrated through her, and the least sigh that escaped from the bloodless lips. The Virgin was but the indefinitely prolonged Echo of the Passion. She felt her brow for the marks of the thorns; she clasped the palms of her hands. Except when she had to turn her care to the prostrated John. . . .

Here should begin the story of the return of Jesus to the world. But that would be the story of the world itself, until the consummation of time. For the presence of the risen Jesus still remains; one would be tempted to say that his Ascension did not interrupt it. Several months after the disciples had seen him disappear he blinded his enemy Saul with his light on the road to Damascus, and spoke to him. Now St. Paul never doubted that he was a witness of the Resurrection in the same way as those who drank and ate with the Christ, victorious over death. This is shown by the famous passage of the First Epistle to the Corinthians, "For I delivered to you before all else, what I also had received, that Christ died for our sins according to the scriptures, and that he was buried, and that he rose on the third day according to the Scriptures; and that he appeared to Kephas, and then to the Twelve. After that he appeared to more than five hundred brethren at once, most of whom still survive, though some have fallen asleep. After that he appeared to James, and then to all the Apostles. Last of all as to one born out of due time, he appeared also to me."

And doubtless the apparitions of Christ which were the guarantees of his Resurrection should not be confused with those with which many souls have been favoured since his ascent into heaven. This does not prevent him who overwhelmed Paul on the road to Damascus from being the same Jesus who was touched, heard and seen by a Francis, a Catherine, a Theresa, a Margaret Mary, a Curé d'Ars, and many saints known and unknown, those proclaimed by the Church and those leading a life of hidden holiness. This Presence is not the Eucharistic Presence, but the little Host gives an idea of it to the most ordinary Christian, when back in his place after Communion, he closes his cloak around that flame in the interior of his being, round the palpitation of Love captive in his heart.

And this is so true that when many Gospel relations seem unimaginable to us, there is none closer to our proven experience than that which treats of the risen Christ. And this first because with us, too, he is only known through his Passion. If he does not reach us from the depths of death he always reaches us from the depths of his suffering. To reach each one of us he ceaselessly journeys through this human hell. His face as we know it is not that of the Jew who, without the kiss of Judas, would not have been recognised by the soldiers of the cohort and the servants of the high priest. It is the Face buffeted and wounded because of our crimes: it is this sad and passionate look which follows us along the course of our life, from fall to fall, without there ever being a lessening or withdrawal of that enveloping love.

There is no meeting of Christ with one of his followers which does not recall to the Christian some event in his own life. Outside the sepulchre Mary Magdalene wept because, "They have taken away the Lord out of the tomb, and we know not where they have laid him." Having said these words she turned and saw Jesus standing, and she did not know that it was Jesus. He said to her, "Woman, why weepest thou? Whom seekest thou?" She, thinking that it was the gardener, said to him, "Sir, if thou hast carried him away, tell me where thou hast laid him, and I will remove him." Jesus said to her, "Mary!" and the eyes of the holy woman opened wide. She said "Rabboni!" We too, have sometimes recognised him. Why not admit it? In his priests very often. We so often speak ill of priests! And yet, the Christian who has the habit (perhaps bad) of kneeling in confessionals here and there, sometimes happens to hear the unexpected and overwhelming word, to receive suddenly from a stranger who is meek and humble of heart, prisoner of that grilled box, the gift of divine tenderness, of a consolation which does not come from man.

How many times has the cry of Thomas, called Didymus, come to our lips, when we too with the eyes of faith, with the outstretched hands of a blind man have seen and touched the wounds of the Lord! *"Dominus meus et Deus meus . . ."* My Lord and my God. He is the possession of all, delivered over to each one of us in particular.

The first time Jesus returned he entered into the room where the disciples were barricading themselves for fear of the Jews. He showed them his wounds: he flooded them with his peace and joy and gave them power to remit sins (oh, the certainty of being pardoned! the hand of the priest on our brow, the words of deliverance which flow over our heart and flesh, like the water and blood from the side opened by the lance!). Thomas was not with them when Jesus came, and he did not wish to believe what they told him. "Unless I see in his hands the print of the nails, and put my finger into the place of the nails, and put my hand into his side, I will not believe." After eight days Jesus came suddenly, and said to Thomas, "Reach hither thy finger, and see my hands, and reach hither thy hand and put it into my side: and be not unbelieving, but believing." Thomas answered him, "My Lord and my God." Jesus said to him, "Because thou hast seen me, Thomas, thou hast believed: blessed are they that have not seen and have believed."

Lord, whom we have not seen with the eyes of the flesh, we believe in thee!

Who among us does not know the inn at Emmaus? Who has not walked on this road one evening when all seemed lost? Christ was dead within us. They had taken him from us—the world, the philosophers and sages, our passions. There was no Jesus for us on the earth. We followed a road, and Someone walked at our side. We were alone and we were not alone. It was evening. Here was an open door, the obscurity of a room where the flame from the fireplace lighted only the trampled earth and made the shadows move. O bread that was broken? O breaking of the bread, consummated despite so much misery. "Stay with us . . . the day declineth. . . ."

The day declineth, life is finishing. Childhood seems further away than the beginning of the world: and of lost youth we hear only the last groaning of the dead trees in some strange wood.

"And they drew nigh to the village whither they were going, and himself made as though he would go further, and they pressed him, saying, Stay with us, for evening approacheth and already the day declineth." So he went in to stay with them. And it came to pass when he had reclined at table with them that he took the bread and blessed and brake and handed it to them. And their eyes were opened, and they recognised him; and he vanished from them. And they said one to another, 'Was not our heart burning within us whilst he spoke to us on the way, whilst he laid open to us the scriptures?' "

Another time Kephas, Thomas, Nathanaël, James and John were fishing. They had come back to their Sea of Tiberias, to their boat, to their nets. ("They have settled down," their families must have thought.) They caught nothing. A stranger told them to cast down their nets on the right side. They caught so many fish that John suddenly understood. "It is the Lord! Peter, it is the Lord!" And Peter immediately cast himself in the sea the sooner to reach his Beloved. He was there, upon the shore. It was indeed he. Some embers were smoking. The sun dried Peter's garments. They cooked their fish; they ate of the bread that Jesus gave them, and they did not even ask: Who art thou? One was never entirely certain that it was he. But yes, my God, it was thou, it was indeed thou who asked the question (how familiar it is to us! but, alas, the answer is not):

"Simon, son of John, lovest thou me more than do these?"

"Yea, Lord, thou knowest that I love thee. . . ."

"Feed my lambs. . . ."

Three times this dialogue passed back and forth on the shore of the lake. Then Jesus moved off a little way and Peter followed him, and John a little after him—as if he had lost his privileged place of the "most loved," as though the risen Lord no longer gave way to the preference of his heart. Nevertheless, he uttered to the son of Zebedee those mysterious words which were to make the other disciples believe that John would not know death. And when, several weeks later, Jesus tore himself from the midst of his disciples, ascended, and was dissolved in light, it was no final departure. Already he was lying in ambush at the turn of the road which went from Jerusalem to Damascus, watching for Saul, his beloved persecutor. Thenceforth in the destiny of every man there was to be this God who lies in wait.

THE END

HARDLY WAS THIS BOOK PUBLISHED when the author wished he could withdraw it, especially since it treats of the only subject that really matters, and also the only one which it is impossible to treat successfully. Too late! Thousands were reading it, and already their protests and reproaches, much the same in nature, were coming from the four corners of the globe. They make the author wonder, "Perhaps it is true that Jesus showed his mother more tenderness than I suggested. And then, in order to describe his physical aspect, had I the right to ignore that document, the Holy Shroud of Turin? Had I the right to substitute for this imprint a personal image which I constructed for myself according to certain ideas of a psychological order, certainly not of a mean or ugly work-man, but of a Galilean like all the others, indeed as Rembrandt saw him? Now, the man scourged and crucified, the man with the pierced heart, who is revealed by the photograph of the Turin relic, was very large and his visage as shown there may well be that which will appear one day in the parted clouds of heaven, in the midst of great majesty and glory. . . . And why did I take away all contour from the face of Mary Magdalene?"

On these points and on several others I have therefore attempted to recast certain parts of the book in the narrow measure that was possible without remodelling my whole work. I must also beg forgiveness of the Biblical scholars whom I have irritated; but it was not my object to attempt any criticism of the texts. The New Testament as it is presented to us to-day is the story of a man with definite traits, of whom each one of us can attempt the psychological portrait. I wished to show that "this document

breathes" as Claudel says, and that in no other story do we feel anyone really live as in this story.

It is not that I mistrust historical criticism, nor that I am
entirely unfamiliar with it. I left college at the height of the crisis
concerning Modernism. The faith of a young Catholic in the
first years of the century was assailed from every quarter. The
Combes persecution was as nothing compared to the attacks
against doctrine, of which the most powerful were led with
diabolical talent and verve from within the Church itself.

He who was still called the Abbé Loisy published nothing which
I did not read with avidity. Certain of his qualities touched me
deeply; when, for example, he said that he did not share that
notion of science which was approved by his superiors, I took him
at his word, and to add my part to the holocaust I sacrificed those
verses of the Gospel which the learned Abbé denounced as inter-
polations. Shall I confess that because of him and his followers
I abstained for years from reading the fourth Gospel and even
among the Synoptics I rarely strayed beyond the text of Mark?

Like many troubled Catholics in those days, difficulties of an
historical order inclined me to seek elsewhere than in history the
foundations of a belief to which I still adhered. Christ, living in
the Church, living in the saints, and in each one of us, made real to
me the Christ of history. At about that time I became an assiduous
reader of the *Annales de philosophie chrétienne*. Interior revelation,
without substituting itself for the historic fact of the Incarnation,
should suffice, I thought, to nullify the hair-splitting of historians.
In my notes I have found numerous citations from Father Tyrrell
and the apologists of Immanence.

Since that time the Church has separated among them the good
grain from the chaff. As for myself, I affirm that from this quarter
much light came to me, and that far from estranging me from the
Christ of Nazareth, the interior study of Christ brought me back
to him. It was a knowledge of the river which relieved me from all
anxiety concerning its source; it was the great spreading tree, its

branches filled with many birds, which made me accept without question the grain of mustard-seed.

Little by little I accustomed myself to a closer examination of certain objections. It was evident that M. Loisy and his disciples used as a point of departure an *a priori* as exacting as my faith could possibly be: the impossibility of admitting anything on the historical plan which might implicate the existence of the supernatural. This negation still gives rise to the most gratuitous suppositions, the most hazardous conjectures. Were I indifferent in these matters I should judge to-day that orthodox criticism has at least in its favour a tradition on which to base itself, whereas the contradictory opinions of its adversaries, save on several unessential points, are no more than points of view and are brought forward only for the purposes of controversy.

"How many efforts are made to obscure the divinity of Christ," as Paul Claudel puts it, "to veil this unbearable visage, to nullify that fact on which Christianity is based, to efface its contours under swathings of erudition and doubt! The Gospel considered in small separate sections constitutes nothing more than a mass of suspicious and incoherent materials in which every amateur seeks of the elements of a construction as pretentious as it is provisional."

When to-day I happen to read over the writings which troubled me, or others more recent, I see clearly that I am dealing with people of passionate convictions, with adherents of an imperious belief. They feel the need of assurance that Jesus was a man like others, an agitator like many before him and many after. But it would have been better, and certainly much more reassuring, if he had never been born. Yes, it would have been better if this man had never been born! Then those who betrayed him could sleep on in peace, their faces turned toward nothingness.

The absence of serenity among certain professional exegetes, their impassioned arguments, their demonstrations made with trembling voice—their very emotions render testimony to him they can slay only for themselves, but who persists in surviving, in shaping the lives of millions of beings. Though I do not even know the name of a certain professor, the tone of his diatribe against my book was enough for me to guess whence the man came, and what black robe he had shed.

To such as these I would say: You cannot speak of him with detachment any more than I can myself. You are engaged in a struggle. You are one of the witnesses of him you are trying to destroy.

The revelation of the Face shown on the Shroud of Turin is but the sensible sign of an even more astonishing miracle: for more than a century this visage has remained intact under the venomous blows of critics; ceaselessly combated, this inextinguishable fire continues to smoulder on in the human forest. The adversaries go to the extreme negation, deny that such a man as Jesus ever existed, denounce in his history a myth born of human hope. They talk, they write, but he is always there, designated by the very blows which rain down upon him. "Where the body shall be," it is written, "there also shall the vultures be gathered together." The vultures are not the only ones who press about the body of the Risen One. . . .

But I know the weakness of my work. After having received so many articles and so many letters I do not doubt that if I have not deformed Christ, I have at least made light and shadow play upon him in accordance with my own obscure preferences. I have stressed those things which correspond to my own preoccupations, and especially the fury of the Man-God, before which my mind really falters—as though I wished to prove to myself that this does not try my faith. That sharpness and violence I have attached to perhaps a too human idea of love; I believe that in Christ they are not opposed to love, that on the contrary they are its indications.

And then in that debate which crops up on every page of my book, and which has to do with the question of Grace, it may be that I have leaned to one side, taking too much away from man and leaving all initiative to Jesus, basing my position in this matter upon the declaration of his sovereign preference: "Ye have not chosen me, but I have chosen you." All the contradictions of the Gospel are solved if we accept the idea that God who is Love yields only to those reasons of the heart which escape from reason.

Just as in a work of human genius each one of us cuts out a kingdom to his own measure, each Christian seeks his own saviour in Christ; and the miracle is that having come for each one of us, we discover among all his words those which are addressed to us in particular—whereas others which touch more lofty souls are better understood by those whose difficulties do not resemble our own or our own secret torments.

But despite the too personal image which the author had made of Christ, he knows that his book has had the good fortune to disturb some sleeping consciences. We who are reluctant to speak of him when our life is so bound up with the world which Christ detested, we must let our thoughts dwell upon this truth, proved by experience: it is as if each Christian had his own plot laid out for him in the Father's land, and each plot must be worked and sowed. If we fail, the essential part of our task is accomplished through us and sometimes despite us. Grace makes use of us just the same for a purpose which is greater than ourselves; it is as if the author of a drama whispers to the bad interpreter of a rôle who speaks his lines indistinctly and haltingly; in the end it is as if, without the knowledge of the public, the author had substituted himself for the actor who has failed. The success obtained is far from what it would have been had the actor succeeded, but in the end certain hearts are reached through him. . . .

The success obtained by this book before a vast audience shows what is badly described as "the actuality of Christ." The events of the present day in history help us to penetrate to the meaning of the mysterious question put by Christ himself and left unanswered by him, "Yet, shall the Son of Man when he cometh, find faith upon the earth?" To-day we see

N

what he will doubtless find: a preparation for faith in the quasi-absence of all positive belief, an extraordinary receptiveness of the human soul. The harassed multitude who, without a leader, flock through the avenues of the great capitals, tramping along behind the various signs and banners, are wasting in the service of fly-by-night doctrines a treasure of disinterestedness and love sufficient to gain eternal life for themselves on that day when he who is Life will appear, and say, "It is I, fear not."

What emboldened me more than anything else to write this Life was just that need of finding again, of touching in some way the living and suffering Man whose place is empty in so many hearts—the Word made flesh, that is, an earthly being, of the same flesh as our own. Certain of those who disagree with me (among others M. Eduoard Dujardin) are surprised that I do not share their temptation to spare Jesus the abasement of an earthly condition, and to accord him a life which is entirely spiritual. For such as Couchoud, as Dujardin, are not blasphemers; nor properly speaking are they atheists. They refuse an historical existence to the Saviour only in order to make him independent of all that could limit, humiliate or detract from God.

Although such a temptation has never presented itself to me, on this point I have succumbed to a requirement of my mind which the concrete alone can satisfy. Shall I admit it? If I had not known Christ, "God" for me would have been a word devoid of meaning. Without a very particular grace, the infinite Being would have been unimaginable and unthinkable to me. The God of philosophers and sages would have had no place in my moral life. For me to believe it was necessary for God to clothe himself in humanity, and at a certain moment of history, on a certain point of the globe, for a human being made of flesh and blood to pronounce certain words and perform certain actions. Then only could I bend the knee. If Christ had not said, "Our Father . . ." I should never of myself have had this sense of sonship; that invocation would never have risen from my heart to my lips. I believe only in what I touch, in what I see, in what is embodied in the same substance as myself—and that is why I believe in Christ. All efforts to minimise the human element in him violate my deepest instincts, and doubtless to this tendency must be attributed my obstinacy in preferring to the visage of Christ the King, of a triumphant Messiah, that humble and tortured face of the man in the inn at Emmaus recognised by Rembrandt's pilgrims when the bread was broken—our brother covered with wounds, our God.

Finally I admit never having entertained that state of mind of those men who call themselves Catholic but who at the same time do not permit themselves to believe in a real Christ. If I did not believe in the words of a certain man born under Augustus and crucified in the reign of Tiberius, if the whole Church rested on a dream or on a lie (and the two are the same in my eyes), its dogmas, its hierarchy, its discipline, its liturgy, would be deprived of all value and even of all beauty: its beauty is the splendour of the real. If Jesus were not the Christ, then I would feel only an immense emptiness in his cathedrals. In case of war the fate of the stained glass of Chartres which justly concerns all persons of good taste would mean less to me than the life of the most humble soldier in the ranks.

An artist who is an unbeliever considers the noble and impressive façade which the Church shows to the world: he admires the Church of Peter, unchanged throughout the centuries. But he forgets the many sacrificed lives, the immolations, which are at its foundation. From generation to generation throughout the ages, the better part of humanity has willingly placed itself upon the cross, and has remained there, and no amount of mockery has brought it down from those heights. No consideration of moral, esthetic or social order would make me accept the crucifixion of so many creatures if Jesus of Nazareth were not the Christ, the Son of God—if he had never existed.

Monasteries and presbyteries (to speak only of monks and priests) are not only filled with joyous souls, filled with abundant spiritual consolations, but these souls enjoy a peace which is not obtainable in the world. Their joy is the fruit of a continual victory over nature, of a very painful victory. And then there are the others: the faithful who remain midway, who struggle, succumb, lift themselves up, fall again, and drag themselves again once more along a road marked by the blood of all those who have gone before them. Sinners and saints, all have believed in a word and have placed their trust in the solemn affirmation, "Heaven and earth shall pass away, but my words shall not pass away." Saints and sinners, all have cried out in moments of doubt and sorrow, "Lord to whom shall we go? Thou hast the words of everlasting life." They care nothing for what the dead have done! What matters to them the dust of those they have not loved! For them it is not a question of accepting a national heritage nor of simulating faiths in legends which help to maintain certain useful virtues. If the impossible were to happen, and it were to be revealed to them that the Son of Man is not the Son of God, they would not continue to follow him, they would no longer bear his cross—even were it for the salvation of a certain civilisation, of a certain culture. They follow him because he said, "I am the Christ . . ." and they believe his words.

It may be objected that hope without foundation is none the less hope, and that if there is no eternity Christians will never know it, and that finally nothingness can confound no one. This reasoning would hold good only for those who leave the world after the world has left them, for those who bring to God the remains of what no one else wants. Yes, for such as these, Pascal's wager will surely be won. But for the others? For all those young beings consecrated to God in the strength and tenderness of youth? They have indeed renounced a reality; human happiness, no matter how imperfect, really does exist. Love seems precarious and ridiculous to us only because it is but a caricature of the divine union. If that union were a snare, if the eternal promises had never rung out in the world, this earthly love would be the pearl without price, for which everything else should be renounced. But the Word was made flesh. The cross is adored only because he was nailed to it. The cross without the Word would have been only a gallows.

And this is why a believer, however weak, however ill-qualified he feels himself to be, is in duty bound to reply to the eternal question: "And what sayest thou of this Man?" This book, so unworthy of its subject, is but one reply among thousands of others, the testimony of a Christian who knows that what he believes is true.

The great tree of Catholicism seems beautiful to us only because it is really living, because despite its dead branches it is flowing with sap, and the blood of Christ continues to circulate from its roots to its least twig and to the last leaf. Catholicism without Christ would be an empty shell curiously wrought. As it is, if a tidal wave were to destroy its temples and cloisters, its palaces and works of art, in reality nothing would be destroyed, since there would remain the Lamb of God whose image I have so faultily drawn.

I insist again that I do not pretend to impose this image on anyone. If each one of our friends imagines us in a way that is different from the others, how much more likely is this to happen when the subject is the Son of God! For this reason I consider I have been granted an unexpected favour in having this Life reach so great a number of souls. I am grateful to the many readers who have shown me they were touched by it. Anonymous letters are not always dastardly; they may be sublime—such as the one which is signed, "*A poor unknown priest whose name would mean nothing to you.*"

Paris,
  August 6, 1936